From Immigrants to Ethnics:
THE ITALIAN AMERICANS

From Immigrants to Ethnics:
THE ITALIAN AMERICANS

Humbert S. Nelli

OXFORD UNIVERSITY PRESS
Oxford · New York
1983

Copyright © 1983 Humbert S. Nelli

Library of Congress Cataloging in Publication Data
Nelli, Humbert S., 1930–
From immigrants to ethnics.

Bibliography: p.
Includes index.
1. Italian Americans—History. I. Title.
E184.I8N44   1983   973'.0451   82-14505
ISBN 0-19-503200-4

Printing: 9 8 7 6 5 4 3 2 1

Printed in the United States of America.

For my son, Chris

Preface

In the era of large-scale immigration before World War I, Italian immigrants generally were the objects of prejudice and contempt. Thus a railroad-construction boss appearing before a Congressional committee in 1890 was asked: "You don't call . . . an Italian a white man?" "No, Sir," the surprised construction boss responded to what seemed a silly question, "an Italian is a Dago."[1]

Italians and their descendants worked successfully to overcome the stigma of being "a Dago," a "Greaseball," an unskilled, unlettered, and poverty-stricken slum dweller, and by the 1980s the vast majority of Italian Americans had become part of the middle class. Nevertheless many of the stereotypes and myths that emerged in the immigrant era have remained.

This book is an effort to present an accurate and balanced picture of the Italian experience in the United States. Part I traces the role of Italians in the discovery and settlement of the New World and in the struggle for American independence from England. It also provides a survey of conditions in Italy that encouraged, if they did not in fact force, millions to leave their homes for the more promising economic opportunities available in the cities of the United States in the decades after 1880. Part II is an examination of various aspects of the immigrant experience, including housing, jobs, politics, community institutions, and the family. Part III traces the emergence of ethnic consciousness among Italian Americans in the postimmigration era.

In the words of sociologist Alfred Aversa, Italian Americans are in search of "a new self-identity."[2] After decades of denying their origins they are proudly, even defiantly, affirming their "Italian-ness." As a group, Italian Americans have completed the transition from immigrant to ethnic rediscovery.

Lexington, Kentucky   H.S.N.
March 1982

Contents

Tables

PART I

BACKGROUND

CHAPTER 1

Early Italians in America

It is a commonplace statement that America was discovered by one Italian (Cristoforo Colombo or, in the latinized form, Christopher Columbus) and named after another (Amerigo Vespucci or Americus Vespucius), but it is based on fact.

On August 3, 1492, Columbus, the "Admiral of the Ocean Sea" (a title later bestowed upon him by Spain's Ferdinand and Isabella), set sail from Palos in southern Spain in the *Santa María* and accompanied by two other ships, the *Niña* and the *Pinta*, to discover a westward passage to the Orient and its wealth. A new era in world history was ushered in on October 12, 1492, when a lookout on the *Pinta* sighted land. It turned out to be an island in the Bahamas which Columbus named San Salvador (or Holy Saviour) and claimed in the name of Spain.

"Other discoveries," Samuel Eliot Morison observed, "have been more spectacular than that of this small, flat sandy island that rides out ahead of the American continent, breasting the trade winds." The significance of the event was, however, far greater than the extent of land sighted or explored, for "it was there that the Ocean for the first time 'loosed the chains of things' as Seneca had prophesied" more than 1000 years before, and "gave up the secret that had baffled Europeans since they began to inquire what lay beyond the western horizon's rim."[1]

Although in this and three subsequent voyages Columbus failed to find his passage to Asia, his contribution, as he accurately noted before his death, was great: "I have placed under the sovereignty of the King and Queen an Other World, whereby Spain, which was reckoned poor, is to become the richest of all countries."[2]

Ironically, the "Other," or New, World that the Genoa-born Columbus discovered for Spain, was eventually named after someone else. Although Vespucci did participate in voyages to the New World, the first in 1499, he never commanded an expedition nor did he personally discover anything. In this case, however, what Vespucci wrote was more important than what Columbus actually accomplished. Letters from Vespucci describing his voyages were printed in his native Florence in 1504–5. They contained a claim that Vespucci had captained a voyage in 1497 that had discovered a new continent. As Vespucci put it: "I have found a continent with a greater multitude of people and animals than our Europe or Asia or Africa."[3] This claim is disputed by Clemente Markham, the editor of an English edition of Vespucci's letters: "The evidence against Vespucci is cumulative and quite conclusive. His first voyage (in 1497) is a fabrication. He cannot be acquitted of the intention of appropriating for himself the glory of having first discovered the mainland."[4] Nevertheless, Vespucci's claim of discovery won almost immediate acceptance as fact, and use of the name "America" for the "New World" quickly spread throughout Europe.

In the meantime Columbus had returned to Spain, a man despised and ignored in his last years of life and who, without realizing it, had opened a new age in European exploration and exploitation. Columbus considered Vespucci a friend and "little suspected that Vespucci's predated account of his voyage with [Spanish captain Alonso de] Hojeda, just published as Mundus Novus, would cause the Florentine to be hailed as the discoverer of a New World, or that in consequence of this faked-up narrative the world of Columbus' discovery would be named America."[5]

Most of the nations of Western Europe participated in and benefited from the ensuing scramble for colonies. Italy, which during the centuries of European colonization of America was a welter of competing city-states, did not possess the wealth of resources necessary to establish and maintain overseas colonies. Owing at least in part to a failure "to constitute a national state like contemporary France and Spain" by 1500, Italy "was about to drift into a period of somnolence during which she lost her commercial and cultural primacy."[6]

The Italian city-states were unable or unwilling to cooperate in any project that might have been mutually beneficial. Therefore while native-born Italians widened the scope of knowledge Europeans possessed of the New World, they did so for the benefit of foreign nations that possessed the foresight and the resources to finance their explorations. Thus the first European expedition to North America was led by an Italian named Giovanni Caboto, or John Cabot. With a crew of eighteen men Cabot set sail from Bristol in May 1497 in his small ship the *Mathew*. Once across the Atlantic, Cabot "touched at Cape Breton [Island], explored the coast of Nova Scotia, and came within sight of Newfoundland, and the next year he sailed south along the coast as far as Chesapeake Bay."[7] All subsequent English claims in North America were based on the travels and the discoveries of the Genoa-born Cabot. Unfortunately, "like Columbus, he never learned the significance or value of his discoveries," for on his second voyage to the New World Cabot and the four ships he commanded disappeared without a trace.[8]

The French followed in the wake of the English and under the guidance of their own Italian navigator, Giovanni da Verrazano, in 1524 sought to discover a northern passage to the Indies. The Florentine and his fifty-man crew never found the passage but he did explore New York harbor eighty-five years before Henry Hudson supposedly discovered it. Verrazano, on his ship *La Dauphine*, was also the first European to enter Narragansett Bay and to round Cape Cod and to "prove that the coast between Florida and Newfoundland belonged to a completely New World." On the negative side, Verrazano was "singularly incurious" and passed up opportunities to explore bays "such as the Chesapeake, the Delaware, and the Hudson estuary, leaving them for the English,

Dutch, and Swedes to explore and colonize in the following century."[9]

In the seventeenth century Enrico Tonti, or Henri di Tonty, explored the Mississippi River basin with Robert Cavalier de la Salle who claimed for his sovereign, Louis XIV of France, the Mississippi and all its tributaries, a region so vast it defied the imagination. Tonti served and explored with La Salle from 1679 until 1687. On March 18, 1687, while on an expedition near the Brazos River in Texas, La Salle's small command mutineed and murdered him. Tonti, who was at the time in Arkansas, was appointed commander of much of the Mississippi region until his own death in 1703. Other members of the Tonti family also served the French Crown with distinction. Enrico's younger brother Alfonso was a cofounder of Detroit and its commander for twelve years. Alfonso's son Henry became governor of Fort St. Louis, while a cousin commanded posts in Illinois.

In the West at least eight of the priests who founded the Spanish Missions in Lower California and Arizona were Italians. The most remarkable of this dedicated and hard-working group was Father Eusebio Chino (or Chini or Kino). Chino was born at Segno near Trento in 1645. In 1687 he arrived in northern Mexico to begin missionary work among the Indians. Over the next twenty-four years, until his death in 1711, he traveled tirelessly on horseback or on foot exploring the Colorado, Gila, Sonora, San Pedro, Santa Cruz, and Altar rivers. "At least twenty southwestern cities," historian Andrew Rolle has noted, "owe their origins to this indefatigable traveller."[10] Chino also established some twenty missions in northern Mexico and what is now the state of Arizona. In addition he was the first person to prove that Lower California was a peninsula and not an island. The "Padre on Horseback," as his biographer Herbert E. Bolton called him, was truly a prodigious worker. He made some fifty trips of a hundred to a thousand miles in distance and regularly covered twenty-five to seventy-five miles a day. "One of the great strengths" of Chino, according to historian Charles Gibson, "and one of the major reasons for his success was his tolerance of existing Indian practices."[11] Chino was not, however, unique in his dedication or his capacity for hard work. It is impossible to determine the exact number of Italian priests at work in the Southwest, but they were numerous and they provided an invaluable service to the Catholic Church and the Spanish Crown in the seventeenth and eighteenth centuries.

In 1610, just three years after the founding of the English colony at Jamestown, Virginia, Italian craftsmen were invited across the Atlantic to provide needed skills. In the early 1620s another small group, this time of four glass-makers, was brought from Venice to Jamestown to set up a glass works to make beads for trade with the Indians. The men soon became unhappy with the conditions they found in the New World. Although two of them decided to remain in Virginia the glass-works project soon ended in failure. Nevertheless, in the following decades Italian craftsmen continued to travel to America. They settled in Virginia and other English colonies, including Rhode Island, Connecticut, Pennsylvania, Maryland, South Carolina, and Georgia. Maryland, which had been founded under Catholic auspices, made a special effort to attract Italians and other European Catholics by the generous offer of land for settlement. Although some skilled workers did migrate, there was never a substantial Italian element in the colony's population. In the final analysis, economic opportunities were much more important than similarities in religion to Northern-Italian Catholics.

A highly skilled group of silk workers from Piedmont, in Northern Italy, migrated in the 1730s to General Oglethorpe's newly founded colony of Georgia. Initially the new silk industry in Savannah enjoyed great success, but it could not meet the challenge of competition from the north and in less than sixty years it disappeared. Some Italians remained in Georgia, but most either followed the silk industry as it relocated in Pennsylvania, Connecticut, and elsewhere in the north, or they returned to Europe.

One group of Northern Italians that did journey to the New World for religious reasons was a Piedmontese Protestant sect called the Waldensians. In 1655 a two-century-long effort by Italian authorities to force the Waldensians to renounce beliefs that Catholics regarded as heretical and to return to the teachings of the Church erupted into violence and many of the Protestants were massacred. Survivors streamed from Piedmont to Protestant nations in Europe. One group accepted an offer from the Dutch government of free transportation to the New World. In the early spring of 1657 the Italians landed in the Dutch colony of New Amsterdam (later to become the English colony of New York). It is not clear whether the Waldensians remained in New Amsterdam or moved to Delaware, which at the time was another Dutch colony. Late in the century another exodus of Waldensians was again directed to the New World, this time to the English colony of Virginia.

Although Italian contacts with colonial America were more numerous than is generally assumed, the numbers involved were small. The largest group of Italian settlers, the Waldensians in New Amsterdam, totaled fewer than two hundred people. Thus the early Italian experience in America is essentially that of a handful of prominent and successful individuals. The most important contributions made by Italians in America during the Revolutionary War era were rendered by Giuseppe Maria Francesco Vigo and Filippo Mazzei.

In the eighteenth century Vigo accumulated a fortune from fur trading with the Indians and gained a reputation as an explorer for his contributions to the opening of the Old Northwest for settlement. Vigo was born at Mondovi in Piedmont on December 3, 1747. At an early age he ran away from home and eventually enlisted in the Spanish army for service in the New World. He served in Havana, Cuba, New Orleans, and St. Louis. Following his discharge in St. Louis Vigo and a fellow Italian, Emiliano Yosti, entered the fur trade and with the aid of a silent partner, Don Fernando de Leyba, the Spanish Governor of St. Louis, became the leading merchants and fur traders in the region. Vigo's operations extended from Detroit to New Orleans and from St.

Louis to Pittsburgh and Montreal. His success was aided in no small measure by his skills as a linguist. In addition to his native language he learned Spanish, French, English, and a variety of Indian tongues, including Chicasaw, Chochtaw, and Shawnee, all of which he spoke perfectly.

In the course of his work Vigo made the acquaintance of a number of American colonists and formed a warm personal friendship with one of the colonists, George Rogers Clark, which helped influence the course of the American Revolution in the West. "Of the many true friends General Clark made amongst the Creoles in the Illinois towns and Vincennes [Indiana]," Clark biographer Temple Bodley observed, "none was more loyal to him, or was a worthier man, than Francis Vigo."[12]

When in 1778 Revolutionary War fighting spread to the Old Northwest Vigo decided to join forces with his close friend General Clark, who was commander of the American forces in the West. In the following years Vigo used his fortune to provide arms and supplies for the colonists and his friendship with various Indian tribes to secure their support for the American cause. Thus historian James G. Randall noted that the Italian not only "furnished large supplies out of his own stores" but also "advanced money to the local inhabitants for the goods which they furnished to the troops." In fact, Randall observed, "without Vigo's ready cash, it is doubtful whether the inhabitants would willingly have parted with their provisions."[13]

Until the end of the war Vigo worked diligently with Clark and his forces to win control of the Northwest. On December 18, 1778, Vigo set off from the Patriot-held town of Kaskaskia for Vincennes to obtain ammunition and other much-needed provisions for Clark's forces. Unknown to Vigo or to Clark, who sent him on the mission, a British force under the command of General Henry Hamilton, one of the ablest British officers in the New World, had arrived from Detroit and retaken the strategic town. Vigo was captured by Indians friendly to England and brought to Vincennes. Vigo was a Spanish subject, and although Hamilton strongly suspected his captive's motives, conventions of the period prevented Vigo's imprisonment. Therefore on Vigo's promise not to escape he was granted the freedom to roam the fort at will.

Vigo carefully observed and committed to memory information concerning fortifications, living conditions, and anything else that might prove of value to Clark when and if he was able to return to Kaskaskia. The French inhabitants of the town, who greatly admired the Italian, pressured Hamilton to release him. Under threat from the townspeople that they would provide no further supplies for the British garrison, Hamilton offered to let Vigo leave the fort if he would sign an agreement "not to do any act during the war injurious to the British interests." Vigo adamantly refused. A compromise finally was worked out by which Vigo agreed "not to do anything injurious to British interests *on his way* to St. Louis," which was the merchant's home.[14]

The agreement was signed and Vigo left Vincennes the next day. Vigo kept to the letter if not the spirit of the agreement. No sooner did he arrive in St. Louis than he set out for Kaskaskia to report on what he had found at Vincennes. On the basis of Vigo's information Clark marched on Vincennes, caught the British forces by surprise, and captured the fort. The February 25, 1779 victory was a key event in the war along the Western frontier. In fact, in the opinion of Judge John Law, who in 1839 published a detailed and insightful history of the Vincennes campaign, "for the immense benefits acquired, and signal advantages obtained by it for the whole Union, it was second to no enterprise undertaken during that struggle." The judge, later a United States Congressman from Indiana, concluded that "the whole credit of this conquest belongs to two men—Gen. George Rogers Clark and Col. Francis Vigo."[15]

During his lifetime Vigo did not receive proper recognition for his contribution to the colonists' cause nor was he repaid for his personal expenditures in financing Clark's expeditions. Although he died unappreciated and a pauper in Indiana on March 22,

1836, Vigo never wavered in his love for the United States, nor did he ever regret his decision to support the Revolutionaries. It was not until 1872, some thirty-six years after Vigo's death, that his claims were acknowledged. By an act of the United States Congress passed on June 8 that year, the demands of his heirs for the money and supplies furnished to Clark and his troops during the Revolution were referred to the Court of Claims. The long, tedious legal process finally ended in May 1876 when the United States Supreme Court ordered payment of the claim which, including interest, totaled $49,898.60 to Vigo's heirs.

Filippo Mazzei, another staunch supporter of the Revolution, was perhaps the best known of the Italians in America during that period. The son of a well-to-do merchant and landowner, Mazzei was born in 1730 near Florence. As a young man he studied medicine and in his free time read in art, politics, and philosophy. He did not complete his medical studies but was issued a certificate enabling him to practice medicine outside of Italy, which Mazzei subsequently did. In the autumn of 1752 he set off for the Near East. For three years, until December 1755, he was a practicing physician in Smyrna, where he first exhibited characteristics that were "to develop and color his whole later life." In Smyrna, his biographer Richard Garlick notes, Mazzei made it a point to cultivate all of the most influential and prominent people: "from then on it was his policy to meet and make friends with those highest in authority and greatest in influence. This partly accounts for the fact that he rose to places of some prominence in so many different localities."[16]

Tiring of the Near East Mazzei sailed to England where he also intended to open a medical practice. His devotion to medicine was not deep and he was soon diverted by business opportunities. Once settled in London he discovered a strong but unsatisfied demand for Italian products, so he began importing wines, olive oil, cheese, candy, and other products from Italy. Although he prospered in his business, he was really more interested in intel-

lectual pursuits. Discourse with his numerous friends held much
more attraction than did the mundane world of economic enterprise.

During the seventeen years he lived in London, Mazzei met and
became friendly with Benjamin Franklin and, through him, with
various other persons from the American colonies. One of them, a
prominent Virginia statesman named Thomas Adams, wrote
Thomas Jefferson about the exceptional Italian who spoke and
wrote so eloquently in support of equality, freedom, and other
ideas that appealed to the colonists. Jefferson, in turn, began a
correspondence with Mazzei which resulted in an invitation to
come to Virginia to set up an experimental farm. The idea that he
would be the first man to plant in America olive and citrus trees,
grape vines for the production of wine, and mulberry trees for the
manufacture of silk strongly appealed to Mazzei's ego. His friend
Benjamin Franklin also strongly encouraged him to go, so in the
fall of 1773, after selling his business in London, Mazzei left for
Tuscany to collect vines, trees, clippings, spades, pruning knives,
and other equipment he would need in Virginia and to recruit ten
peasants to work the farm.

Mazzei and his small band of workers boarded a chartered ves-
sel at Leghorn on September 2, 1773. After a voyage of nearly
three months they landed in Virginia, where Mazzei set off overland with Thomas Adams for Adams's home in Augusta County
where the experimental farm was to be located. On the way they
stopped at Monticello to see Thomas Jefferson. Jefferson suggested
Mazzei buy a 400-acre estate adjacent to his own that was for sale,
and even offered to add 2000 acres of his own land. The Tuscan
followed Jefferson's advice and set up his farm, which he named
Colle.

Mazzei was indirectly responsible for furthering the teaching of
Italian and other European languages in Virginia when he introduced Carlo Bellini to Jefferson. Bellini was an old Florentine
friend who had become dissatisfied with conditions in Italy. A few
months after Mazzei emigrated, Bellini and six more farm workers

followed him to the New World. Through the help of Jefferson and other prominent Virginians, Bellini became an instructor of modern languages, including Italian, French, and Spanish, at the college of William and Mary—the first teacher of those languages in an American college.

The agricultural experiment at Colle eventually failed, in part because Mazzei increasingly devoted his time and energies to the colonists' growing conflict with England. Farming in Virginia held no more attraction for him than had the conduct of his import business in London or his medical practice in Smyrna. Soon after his arrival Mazzei became deeply involved in local politics.

In 1774 the Italian was one of twelve men elected to represent the voters of Albemarle County in their dealings with the colony's government in Williamsburg. Mazzei was later elected to other local offices and was held in high esteem by the local citizens, but his major contribution to the colonists' cause was less in the arena of practical politics than in the formulation and enunciation of ideas. At Jefferson's suggestion Mazzei prepared a series of articles in 1774 and 1775 which presented the philosophical justifications for a revolution against England. The articles, written in Italian, were translated by Jefferson and published under the name "Furioso" in John Pinckney's *Virginia Gazette*.

In one of the articles Mazzei expounded ideas and used phrases that may have directly influenced Jefferson when he wrote the preamble of the Declaration of Independence. Mazzei held that "All men are by nature equally free and independent. This quality is essential to the establishment of a liberal government, a truly republican form of government cannot exist except where all men, from the very rich to the very poor, are perfectly equal in their natural rights."[17]

Mazzei also helped revise Virginia's legal code and perhaps had a hand in drafting the first version of the state's constitution of 1776. This contribution to the revolutionary cause was, despite his diligent efforts, at best meager. In 1779, when state officials sent him on a mission to raise funds in Europe for Virginia's war effort, his ship was captured just thirty miles out of port by the English. He eventually made his way to Europe but without documents verifying his claim to represent Virginia. This mission was made even more difficult because Benjamin Franklin undercut his efforts. Franklin, who was in Europe as representative of the Continental Congress, felt that relations between individual states and foreign countries should be conducted through the central government. Thus even with his documents Mazzei would probably have had a difficult time raising funds.

The improverished and increasingly disenchanted agent remained in Europe for three years attempting to aid the American cause by whatever means he could. Mazzei published pro-American propaganda in a Florentine newspaper; wrote a series of personal letters to European leaders; and prepared pamphlets, such as *The Justice of the American Cause, The Importance of Establishing Commercial Relations in Virginia,* and *The Probability of the Successful Outcome of the American Revolution.* He also dispatched a steady stream of informative and beautifully written reports to Jefferson, now Virginia's governor, concerning European attitudes and events, but the extent of his influence was limited and his contribution was minimal.

Following the successful conclusion of the American Revolution Mazzei returned to Virginia for the last time. He was showered with praise for his efforts in Europe but not with the diplomatic appointment he hoped to receive. In June 1785, after spending less than two years in his adopted homeland, he set sail for Europe. Mazzei spent the remaining years of his life in Europe, the last twenty-four in his native Tuscany, but he retained his strong interest in the American experiment in government.

On his return to Europe Mazzei settled in Paris where for the next three years he lived in abject poverty because his money was tied up in Virginia real estate and in loans he was unable to collect. With little else to do and because there was at the time no accurate history of the United States available in Europe, he wrote, and in 1788 published, a four-volume study titled the *His-*

torical and Political Origins of the United States of North America. Although acknowledged to be an excellent work it made Mazzei little money.

Fortunately, in 1788 Mazzei found employment as agent in Paris of Stanislaus II, the liberal king of Poland. Although he had no diplomatic status Mazzei received 8000 livres a year as "intelligencer," or secret correspondent, for Stanislaus in the French capital. Just a year after his appointment the French Revolution erupted and, Garlick observed, "Mazzei had the difficult yet intensely interesting duty of reporting it to the King of Poland."[18] Mazzei held high hopes and expectations for the impending revolution and during its early stages attempted to help guide it along the same liberal and moderate course as the American Revolution and was appalled when it soon took a radical and violent direction. His work as intelligencer came to an end in December 1791 when Stanislaus called him to Warsaw to serve as adviser to the king. He departed the country within a year, however, because of the worsening economic and political situation which, in 1793, culminated in the Second Partitioning of Poland by Austria, Prussia, and Russia.

From Poland Mazzei returned to Italy and settled in Pisa where he died in 1816 at the age of eighty-five. When Thomas Jefferson learned of his old friend's demise he wrote the American Consul at Leghorn. Mazzei, Jefferson observed, "had some peculiarities, and who of us has not? But he was of solid worth; honest, able, zealous in sound principles moral and political, constant in friendship, and punctual in all his undertakings. He was greatly esteemed in this country."[19]

Jefferson might also have noted that Mazzei was ever ready to heed the call of his friends for help. Thus when in 1805 Benjamin Henry Latrobe, architect of the Capitol in Washington, D. C., needed to secure a "first rate sculptor" and an assistant "to serve the newly established federal government in erecting public buildings in the capital and to work on the Capitol itself," President Jefferson directed him to write Mazzei for help.[20] As always Mazzei diligently set about finding the best-qualified artists available. Although seventy-five years old at the time, he went to Florence and Rome in an effort to carry out Latrobe's request. The men he sent to America, Joseph Franzoni and John Andrei of Florence, did fine work, as Jefferson reported in a letter to Mazzei in 1807: "the sculptors are here, well in health, well employed, and greatly esteemed."[21] Franzoni and Andrei, for their part, were well pleased with their employment and with life in Washington, and they in turn brought other sculptors from Italy to contribute to the building and decorating of the United States Capitol.

Like Mazzei, settlers in the colonial period generally came from Northern Italy. This pattern continued in the decades between the Revolution and the 1880s, although New York City's Italian colony contained newcomers from all parts of the homeland. By later standards the number of arrivals was quite small. In 1790, for example, New York and Philadelphia were the two largest cities in the nation. Howard Marraro has estimated that in that year New York, with a total of 33,131 people, had only about twenty Italian families while not more than eight Italian families resided among Philadelphia's 28,522 inhabitants. Compared with the mass immigration of unlettered and unskilled peasants and farm laborers this was, according to Marraro, a unique group which included "distinguished travellers, scientists, physicians, musicians, artists, and businessmen."[22] Among the businessmen were merchants, restaurateurs, wholesale and retail liquor dealers, confectioners, shopkeepers, and printers. There was also a sprinkling of tailors and seamstresses, carpenters, and laborers. With relatively few exceptions, little is known about the early immigrants.

In addition to the permanent residents who generally arrived in search of economic opportunity, New York also received a small stream of political refugees during the first half of the nineteenth century. "As men of culture and education," Marraro has noted, "these political refugees readily won places of honor and distinction for themselves in the American business and professional worlds."[23] Although many remained in the United States for years, and some for the rest of their lives, all intended their stay to be temporary and when the political climate in Italy was right they planned to return. Among these champions of independence and national unification for their native land were Luigi Chitti, a prominent economist who served as Minister of Finance in Naples in 1821 and who was twice condemned to death for his revolutionary activitives; Pietro Borsieri, a leader of the Milan *Carbonari* in 1821; Felice Foresti, another prominent *carbonaro*; Quirico Filopanti, secretary of the Roman Republic of 1849; and General Giuseppe Avezzano, vice-president and minister of war of the Roman Republic of 1849.

One of the first exiled Italian nationalists to settle permanently in America was Lorenzo Da Ponte, a Venetian Jew converted to Catholicism who landed in Philadelphia in 1805 at the age of fifty-six. Da Ponte had been librettist for three of Mozart's greatest operas, including *Don Giovanni*. He soon moved to New York where he worked as a grocer, bookseller, and teacher of Italian. In 1825 he became the first professor of Italian language and literature at Columbia University. At the age of eighty-four he was one of the prime movers in the construction of an Italian opera house and the formation of an opera company in New York. Another exile from Italian revolutionary activity, the Sicilian Pietro Bacchi, was appointed professor of Italian at Harvard in the same year Da Ponte assumed his duties at Columbia. A vigorous and active man with wide-ranging interests, Da Ponte lived to the age of ninety. His successor at Columbia was a fellow political exile, Felice Foresti.

The most famous Italian exile was Giuseppe Garibaldi, who was acclaimed by the New York newspapers, on his arrival in 1849, as "the distinguished champion of liberty." According to the New York *Herald* few men "have achieved so much for the cause of freedom, and no one has accomplished so many heroic acts for the independence of a fatherland, as General Garibaldi has for Italy."[24] During his stay Garibaldi lived on Staten Island at the home of a friend, Antonio Meucci, and worked at Meucci's small

candle factory. After nearly a year in New York Garibaldi grew
restless and departed by ship for Latin America. He returned to
Italy in 1859 to play a major role in the unification of the nation.
Garibaldi's host, Antonio Meucci, was a scholar and idealist
"whose claims to be the original inventor of the telephone have
found many supporters."[25] Unfortunately, few of these "supporters" stepped forward while this tragic figure was alive and
needed their help.

In the nearly eight decades from the American Revolution to
the Civil War a number of well-born Italian travelers passed
through New York and other East Coast cities on their journeys
around the country. Thus shortly after the end of the Revolution,
Count Luigi Castiglioni, a renowned naturalist, came to the New
World. The Milanese nobleman traveled in the United States from
1785 to 1787. On his return to Italy Castiglioni presented his
observations on human, plant, and animal life in America in a well-
received two-volume work. Count Paolo Andreani, another visiting
Milanese aristocrat and naturalist, arrived in America in 1790
and traveled along the then Western frontier and was the first
European to circumnavigate Lake Superior. On his return from the
West in 1792 he was elected a member of the American Philosophical Society in Philadelphia.

In the following years an increasing number of Italian travelers
came to America. Like Castiglioni and Andreani, they generally
were well-educated members of the upper class. The story of Italians in America is not, however, of these persons or of other
members of Northern Italy's social and economic elite who came
to the New World as intrepid explorers, champions of American
independence, or exiles from Italian political oppression. It is,
rather, the experience of millions of unskilled and unlettered immigrants, most of whom came from the Southern provinces of
Italy in the decades between 1880 and World War I, and of their
descendants. For these immigrants the story had its start in nine-
teenth-century Southern Italy, the poverty-stricken land of *la
miseria*.

CHAPTER 2

The Land of
La Miseria

More than five million Italians have arrived in the United States since 1820, when American immigration statistics were first kept. The peak period was in the years between 1880 and 1914, the beginning of World War I, when nearly four million Italians arrived. Eighty percent of the immigrants came from the *Mezzogiorno*, the provinces south of Rome and the island of Sicily.

For the vast majority of Southern-Italian peasants, emigration offered the best, perhaps the only, hope for improving their lives. The grandeur and glory of the ancient Roman Empire had long since faded away, and Italy by the nineteenth century was a poverty-stricken land whose only major natural resource was people.

Overpopulation constituted a fundamental and chronic problem in Italy. In 1909 the population density in the Kingdom of Italy was 310 inhabitants per square mile. By the beginning of the twentieth century, among the nations of Europe only Belgium, the Netherlands, and England had greater population densities, and all three—unlike Italy—ranked as highly industrialized nations. Despite a large emigration (3,366,481 between 1881 and 1911), the population continued to grow. In 1881 it was 28 million, in 1901 it was 32 million, and by 1909 it exceeded 34 million. The birth rate was high. During the years between 1904 and 1908 the excess of births over deaths was 1,845,775, or an average of 369,155 for each year of the five-year period. Overpopulation alone, however, did not cause emigration. Seriously compounding Italy's problems was that it was also a very poor country, deficient in the natural resources necessary for industrialization.

Italy attempted to act like a great power without the necessary industrial resources. Unfortunately the nation lacked agricultural as well as industrial resources. Francesco Nitti, a prominent economist and member of the Italian Parliament who later would become Prime Minister of the Kingdom, noted in 1904 that "the territory of Italy is very small, but it is rendered still smaller by the fact that Italy is the most mountainous of the great countries of Europe."[1] More than three-quarters of the land is covered by mountains. Fertile farm land was, and still is, limited in extent, most of it in the northern parts of the peninsula.

The abolition of feudalism in the early nineteenth century, which was intended to benefit the people, and especially the poor, simply reinforced the existing order which was controlled by owners of large estates. The newly created Kingdom of Italy in the years after 1860 seized and sold the vast land holdings of the Catholic Church but instead of helping to improve conditions this simply compounded already existing problems. Nearly all the land was purchased by large landowners or by speculators instead of by the peasants, who could not afford the high purchase prices. The new owners exploited the land and turned heavily forested areas in the South to agricultural use. This in turn resulted in soil erosion and the creation of marshes in the valleys of the South. The marshes, in turn, became breeding places for malaria-carrying mosquitos, which infected at least two million people each year. Because of the menace of malaria, peasants could not live on the land they cultivated as low-lying land was the most malarial as well as the most fertile. It was therefore necessary for the peasants to live in villages and towns in the higher hills and travel to their farms in the valleys, a walk of several miles each day.

Although some of the towns held sizeable populations they were not industrial or commercial centers. That is, they were not urban in the usual sense of the word but rather were residential compounds. The rural towns of the *Mezzogiorno* were, as Carlo Levi has described them in *Christ Stopped at Eboli*, miserable and wretched places in which to live. "The peasants' houses were all alike," Levi wrote, "consisting of only one room that served as kitchen, bedroom, and usually as quarters for the barnyard animals as well, unless there happened to be an outhouse." The only light in the room "was that from the door. The room was almost entirely filled by an enormous bed, much larger than an ordinary double bed; in it slept the whole family, father, mother, and children." Babies were kept in little reed baskets hung from the ceiling. "Under the bed slept the animals, and so the room was divided into three layers: animals on the floor, people on the bed, and infants in the air."[2]

Levi's description was of peasant life in Lucania (or Basilicata) but it applied to the other provinces of the South as well. Writing of the towns in turn-of-the-century Sicily a visitor reported the dwellings of the peasants to be

little more than hovels. They usually have only one room, often windowless, or lighted only by the door, for windows are a luxury in Sicily; good glass is very expensive and cheap glass cracks in the hot sun. The floor is of worn stone, the walls are rudely plastered and the only heat in winter comes from the small charcoal brazier that is used in preparing the food. An iron bedstead, a shaky table, and a few rude chairs cover the furnishings. The walls are decorated with political characters taken from the newspapers, advertisements of steamship lines to the United States and South America, and a wooden crucifix suspended in the corner.[3]

A Calabrian peasant who returned to the town in which he was born after decades of living in the New World found it "impossible to breathe freely" in the home village. "It is dirty; you must always hide something or from some one; every one lies about everything: wealth, eating, friendship, love, God. You are always under the eyes of someone who scrutinizes you, judges you, envies you, spies on you, throws curses against you, but smiles his ugly, toothless mouth out whenever he sees you."[4]

In the nineteenth century Italian observers such as Vincenzo Padula, a priest and poet of some prominence, found peasants in the South living at a bare subsistence level. According to Padula, "the peasant works in order to eat, he eats in order to have the strength to work; then he sleeps. This is his life."[5] Conditions in the *Mezzogiorno* by the 1880s were every bit as bad as those that caused the great migration from Ireland in the 1840s. The land was predominately divided into large estates with absentee landlords and supervision in the hands of overseers. Labor was performed by tenants who employed primitive instruments and practices, exploited the land, and prevented or slowed the introduction of modern machinery and farming methods. The result was a marginal existence. "Add to this the sloth and vileness of the ruling class," a shocked and disgusted Francesco Nitti found, adding that "in some provinces every citizen who can count on 500 or 600 *lire* of annual income thinks himself justified in not working and, as they say, 'lives on his rent.'" In Basilicata Nitti recalled visiting "a wretched village, very poor and miserable from malaria and emigration, in which of a population of about 5000 there were *seventy-two* priests," most of whom were "*living on their rents* with no other occupation than village politics."

The situation in the North began to improve in the latter part of the nineteenth century with the introduction of crop rotation, machinery, and fertilizers. Few modern farming methods penetrated to the South, where the only grain crop was wheat and field workers labored with hoes and spades and occasionally with hand plows. Artificial fertilizers were scarcely known in the South. Obviously, in these circumstances Southern Italy could provide no serious competition for United States, Canadian, or Argentine-grown wheat.

Throughout history Southern Italy was exploited by invaders and conquerors but none victimized the region more than the government of the new Kingdom of Italy controlled by fellow Italians from the North. As far as the Southerner was concerned the foreign domination continued, now in the form of a more efficient, oppressive, and ruthless government in Rome. The South, in fact, "contributed more to government revenues in proportion to its wealth, while at the same time benefiting less from government disbursements in proportion to what it paid."[6]

Unification also dealt a severe blow to Southern industrial development. Prior to 1861 industrialization had progressed almost to the North's level, but in following years governmental policy discriminated against Southern provinces. By the turn of the century the North had made great advances in wealth, trade, and education, while the South remained almost stationary, if it had not, in fact, retrogressed. The reason for the difference in progress could be traced to the government, which lavished favors on the North and promoted its industry and trade by means of protectionist tariffs and other barriers to free trade, while turning its back on the problems and needs of the largely agricultural South. Tariff bills and other legislation enacted by the central government to protect and encourage emerging industry in the North benefited that part of the Kingdom at the expense of the South. In addition, when customs duties between the former Italian states were abolished, the South lost a great deal of revenue that now flowed to Rome.

In the decades following unification, Southern-Italian peasants fell deeper into *la miseria*. A repressive system of taxation and usurious interest rates further undermined whatever initiative remained and discouraged efforts at self-improvement. By the end of the nineteenth century, taxes in Italy were the highest in Europe and weighed especially heavily on those least able to pay, that is, on the *contadini* (peasants) and the *giornalieri* (or day laborers) of the South. Among these were taxes on land, buildings, and on moveable wealth. Excise taxes were placed on salt, sugar, tobacco, liquor, and other items over which the government exercised a monopoly. Some of the taxes, such as that on salt, comprised a very substantial portion of the price of the item. Not only did the central government tax heavily but so did the provinces and the communes. In fact, the bulk of the taxes was levied by the local governments (the communes).

The South also suffered from a series of natural disasters that included earthquakes, droughts, volcanic eruptions, landslides, and plant parasites. The phylloxera plant parasite had a profound effect on the South's economy. The parasite destroyed most of the vineyards of Southern Italy and virtually annihilated the country's wine industry for a time during the 1890s. An immediate result was that French wines began to replace the Italian product in the world market. A longer-term result was the displacement of thousands of farm laborers who turned to emigration as an escape from economic disaster.

Even more damaging, according to historians of Italy, was the lack of rainfall. Some believe that the annual rainfall has declined since ancient times when the South was "the garden of the Roman Empire," and there appears to be some validity in this belief. Of

Table 1. Median Yearly Rainfall in Italy (in Millimeters) 1871–1926

Province	Winter	Spring	Summer	Fall	Total Yearly Rainfall
North					
Piedmont	120.8	265.3	152.6	192.2	731.2
Venetia	139.0	179.3	188.7	227.8	740.6
Liguria	350.9	319.5	179.5	487.7	1,307.4
Tuscany	201.4	215.5	139.7	275.2	822.8
South					
Campania	285.1	196.8	72.0	371.1	873.0
Apulia	208.0	140.3	59.0	219.0	622.6
Sicily	290.7	149.8	32.0	240.6	718.8

Source: Leonard Covello, *The Social Background of the Italo-American School Child* (Leiden, Netherlands, 1967), pp. 35–36. Based on Gaetano Zingali, *Liberalismo e fascismo nel Mezzogiorno d'Italia*, Vol. I, pp. 15–27.

still greater importance, however, is the distribution of the rain that does fall. The total annual precipitation in the South is not significantly lower than that in the North but it falls during the wrong seasons of the year for agricultural purposes. The rainfall in the North is heaviest during the spring and summer when crops need moisture for germination and fruition. By contrast, precipitation in the South is greatest in the fall and winter when, instead of nourishing the earth, it furthers the process of soil erosion. The problem is compounded during the summer months by the lack of irrigation and by the presence of the dry "sirocco" winds. Blowing out of the African deserts and across Southern Italy during the growing season, these winds dry up crops or cover them over with sand and soil.

Another climatic problem affecting agriculture in the South was temperature. Table 2 demonstrates that the South was not only drier than the North but it also was hotter during both the winter and the summer.

Socially and economically Southern Italy was a static, closed society. A rigid caste system existed which made upward socio-economic mobility extremely difficult for the vast majority of the people to achieve. The population was divided between the few

Table 2. Median Temperatures in Italy 1871–1931 (Fahrenheit)

Region	Winter	Summer	Annual	Minimum	Maximum	Differences in Degrees Between Winter and Summer
North	36.38	73.40	55.40	6.62	96.98	36.54
South	52.12	75.20	63.50	38.58	113.90	23.14

Source: Leonard Covello, *The Social Background of the Italo-American School Child* (Leiden, Netherlands, 1967), p. 37. Based on Gaetano Zingali, *Liberalismo e fascismo nel Mezzogiorno d'Italia*, Vol. I, p. 29.

who were wealthy, socially prominent, and politically powerful, and the many, who were poverty-stricken and powerless. "The majority of the great landed proprietors," wrote Englishman Richard Bagot, who traveled extensively through turn-of-the-century Italy, "have never possessed that sense of duty and of responsibility to their tenants and dependents which has almost invariably characterized their counterparts in England."[7] Also, unlike England, the middle class in Italy was virtually nonexistent. Emigration was one of the few means available for ambitious young men to realize some degree of upward social and economic mobility. For the vast majority of Southern-Italian peasants, emigration was "the major source of achievement" available to them.

Among the few domestic means of "making it" were the Catholic Church or criminal organizations such as the Mafia. The Catholic Church was a central element of village life. It served as a social as well as a religious force, and because it exerted a wide-ranging and pervasive influence, the village priest played an important role in the community. Recognizing the opportunities the priesthood offered for improving their social status, some ambitious and intelligent peasant youngsters were attracted to the profession. In the decades after unification, "it was the height of a peasant family's ambition that one of its members should become a priest."[8] The young men entered the clergy and served their parish well. Unfortunately, the number of openings available in the priesthood was limited and upward mobility within the hierarchy of the Church was severely restricted for the lower classes.

A chasm existed between the local clergy, who were often born and raised in the village they served, and the higher officials of the Church. The latter group generally came from upper-class families and in their official capacity in the Church took their place alongside military officers and governmental officials as important members of the state's power structure.

For some peasant youths far greater opportunities existed in crime than in the Church. In a speech before the Italian Parliament in the 1870s, jurist Diego Trajani, himself a Sicilian native, described the situation under the Italian Kingdom: "We have in Sicily [and elsewhere in the South] the laws scoffed at, . . . corruption everywhere, favouritism the rule, justice the exception; crime enthroned where the guardian of public weal should be; . . . By heaven! What is this but chaos; what but the worst of all evils?"[9] Under such conditions as these the Mafia in Sicily, and the *'ndranghita* (*fibbia*) in Calabria, functioned and flourished as an extralegal (and "parallel") form of government.

The secret criminal organizations developed, in large part, in the rural areas of the South. This resulted at least in part because of the prevalence of absentee landlords. The census conducted in 1901 found that two-thirds of the landlords of Sicily and two-fifths of those in Calabria did not live on, cultivate, or manage the property they owned. Absentee landowners hired armed guards to protect their crops and their herds of cattle, as well as to collect rents and intimidate workers. Overseers employed Mafiosi not only to exploit the peasants but also to intimidate the absentee owners in order to rent estates on easy terms.

Over time, these "protectors" became powerful in their own right. For each job performed for landowners or overseers they gained a share of the proceeds. Although they did not usually flaunt their wealth, they enjoyed a higher standard of living than did their compatriots. Instead of earning the hatred of the lower classes, from whose ranks they themselves came, successful Mafia and *fibbia* members enjoyed special prestige in their own locality. In large part, however, this stemmed from the fact that they made themselves "respected." In a land where the mass of people suffered daily humiliation with no redress, Mafiosi, as *uomini rispetati* ("respected men"), suffered insults from no one. In the process they became objects of admiration and envy.

Leaders of both the Mafia and the *fibbia* were men of dignity who commanded respect without demanding it and exerted a profound influence in the local economy and in politics. People brought their problems, such as difficulties with the law, and job and money needs, to the patrons who solved them in return for favors and pledges of support and respect. In the process the patrons accumulated immense power and influence, and although they lived quietly, frugally, and inconspicuously, they also acquired great wealth. Functioning as the friend and champion of the oppressed, the *fibbia*, like the Mafia, also allied itself with local landowners and politicians and exerted a generally decisive influence in elections in exchange for helping to control the local population. As Denis Mack Smith maintained, based on research conducted by Leopoldo Franchetti and Sidney Sonnino in Sicily in 1876, "crime was a means only; the chief object, as always, was to win respect, power and hence money."[10]

In the impersonal and hostile environment that existed in the South the ordinary peasant could place his trust and faith only in the nuclear family—that is, the immediate members of his household. Extended family closeness and supportiveness, an ideal much admired and desired in the Italian South, was seldom attained because of the harsh economic and social conditions. Each person was expected to mind his own business and that of the immediate family, which in the South comprised one and the same thing. Envy, jealousy, and suspicion typified contacts with and attitudes toward the wider family group—aunts and uncles, nieces and nephews, cousins of varying degrees and closeness. The man of the family turned to relatives only when he needed a favor; but because his own prestige increased in proportion to the loss of a relative's prestige, and vice versa, he acted prudently if he did not completely trust kinsmen. A well-known Sicilian proverb with which the vast majority of Southern Italians could agree was that "the real relatives are those inside the house."[11] One was wise, sociologist Joseph Lopreato has noted, not to place too much trust even in nuclear family members for "the nuclear family itself is not free from intense internal conflict."[12]

Although in Southern-Italian and Sicilian villages most residents were related, little closeness, cohesiveness, or feeling of unity existed among the villagers. A sense of community simply did not exist. Southerners had a fierce loyalty to their town, the so-called spirit of *campanilismo* (or localism), but this loyalty was not synonymous with a spirit of group cooperation or acceptance of responsibility for the needs and interests of the community. Residents simply did not recognize "the community," as the term is understood in the United States and elsewhere in Western Europe. "Like so many of the dreams of the *Mezzogiorno*," sociologist Francis Ianni has observed, "the harsh social and economic realities of the region have always kept the vision out of the reach of the peasant and the urban poor."[13]

That this situation has not yet changed was demonstrated in the aftermath of the earthquakes that rocked Southern Italy in 1980. Louis B. Fleming, a European correspondent for the Los Angeles *Times*, found that the quakes revealed a basic flaw in Italian society. "The cynicism, deceptiveness, peccadillos and worse of many politicans are also the characteristics of many of the Italian people," Fleming observed. They are "the fruit of a preoccupation with the individual, the family unit, the immediate circle of friends, at the expense of community, to say nothing of nation." The basic problem, as one prominent Italian acknowledged to Fleming, was that " 'there is simply no sense of community' " in Southern Italy.[14]

The growth of a sense of community among Italian immigrants in the United States was not transplanted but, rather, resulted from settlement in the New World. Similarly, the cohesive, extended family, which was only a dream in Southern Italy, came closer to reality in the immigrant neighborhoods of American cities. Even there, Ianni notes, "the ideal of the closely knit, socially and economically integrated extended family remained illusory" for most of the immigrants, although "for some families, success in business whether legal, illegal or both, allowed them to realize the dream and to use their wealth and power to build a family business patterned on the extended family."[15] The extended family has functioned most effectively, Ianni maintains, in the operation of criminal syndicates in America.

Emigration was a vital safety valve for dissatisfaction and discontent, and the Italian government recognized this fact. It looked upon massive emigration as the easiest and most convenient means of relieving potentially disruptive socio-economic and political pressures in the South. Thus Luigi Bodio, a member of the Italian parliament, stated in 1895 that "emigration is a good thing for the mother country. . . . It is a safety valve, or security against envy and class odium, an efficacious instrument in the equalization of human forces."[16] Legislation passed by parliament in December 1888 proclaimed the right of Italians to emigrate freely from the Kingdom, but the government did little of a substantive nature then or in subsequent years to protect or aid emigrants before their departure, during the arduous ocean voyage, or upon their arrival and settlement in the New World.

The attitude of the Italian government began to change after the passage of a new emigration law in 1901 that was intended to provide more effective protection for emigrants than had earlier legislation and, through the creation of a *Commissariato Generale della Emigrazione* (or Bureau of Emigration), to coordinate and unify services for Italian nationals in other countries. Neither the *Commissariato* nor the 1901 law lived up to the high hopes entertained for them. The government still showed more interest in the money emigrants sent or personally brought back to Italy than in the conditions under which they worked or lived while out of the country. After 1908 Italy entertained grandiose dreams of a vast colonial empire and emigration was a vital element in the plans. Until World War I intervened, Italians were still allowed to leave the country but the emigration was to be "undisguisedly temporary." Italians who journeyed beyond the nation's borders were to keep the homeland ever in their thoughts and were "some day to return," preferably with large amounts of capital earned abroad to pump into the Kingdom's economy.[17]

"Purely economic causes" were responsible for "practically all emigration from Italy."[18] The emigrants were driven by a desire to escape abject and wretched poverty and a vicious system of taxation, the burden of which fell almost exclusively on poor peasants. At the same time they were attracted by the hope of bettering their miserable conditions through seasonal or temporary labor elsewhere in Europe or overseas. In 1882 the Italian government requested provincial officials throughout the country to investigate their jurisdictions and provide accurate information as to the basic factors responsible for emigration from the Kingdom. The answers were nearly unanimous in ascribing emigration to three factors: "destitution, lack of work, and a natural desire to improve their condition."[19]

Despite the numerous factors working to dislodge the peasant from his village as well as the availability of economic opportunities in the New World serving to attract him, Southern Italians, like the Irish in the years before the Great Migration of the 1840s, were reluctant to leave their villages. In fact emigration from Italy began first from the North. Throughout most of the nineteenth century Northern Italians migrated across the Alps to Western and Central Europe or across the Atlantic Ocean to Argentina, Brazil, and other Latin-American countries, although a small number were diverted to the United States, especially to California. The limited emigration from Southern Italy in the years before unification was primarily to North Africa.

The flow of transoceanic migration varied according to the relative economic opportunities available in the receiving countries. The allure of Latin America decreased toward the end of the century, resulting in large part from the unsettled political and financial conditions in Brazil and Argentina. At the same time that economic opportunities for immigrants in Latin America dimished, industrial expansion in the United States required unskilled laborers. Moreover, transportation to the United States cost less than to Latin America and immigrants could earn more money in North America—two important reasons for emigration to the United States.

Italians still felt drawn to Argentina and Brazil, but by the time these countries had settled their immediate political and economic problems the mainstream of Italian migration had been diverted toward the United States. The movement to the United States differed in two respects from that to Latin America: place of origin in Italy and the size of the migration. While Northern Italians comprised some 90 percent of the emigration to Latin America, approximately 90 percent of the migration to the United States was from the Southern provinces. In addition, larger numbers of Italians went to North America than had reached the Latin countries. Rarely had a yearly total of immigrating Italians equaled or exceeded 100,000 in Argentina or Brazil; after 1900 this total was a yearly minimum for the United States and approached 300,000 in 1914, but World War I then intervened to effectively end further migration.

The Southern-Italian adherence to tradition and resistance to movement from the place of origin began to break down in the decades after unification. Emigration did not, however, flow evenly from all parts of the South. It came, rather, from those areas that experienced the breakdown of the old feudal system of class stratification, without compensating working-class organizations such as trade unions and cooperatives. Dissatisfaction with economic conditions, combined with fear of losing status in a society that had previously and traditionally been closed and unchanging, stimulated the desire to emigrate. Thus those who departed were not the dregs, those at the bottom of the economic ladder, but sturdy and hardy peasants who were a step or two up and who feared impoverishment and the loss of status.

In a report to the Department of State prepared in 1886, Edward Camphausen, the American Consul in Naples, reported that "of the peasants, or those cultivating or working the soil, 90 percent are owners of some property, if only consisting of a small house." The fact that emigration offered an important means of upward mobility contributed to the disintegration of feudal-class distinctions. Those who departed came, according to the American Consul in Palermo, Philip Carroll, from "the more frugal, thrifty, and energetic" members of Southern society, a point that was confirmed and repeated by later observers.[20] The Reverend N.

Walling Clark, who was for several years in charge of educational
activities of the Methodist Church in Italy, told the United States
Immigration Commission in 1911 that "the class of emigrants who
go to the United States are unquestionably the more enterprising,
the better element; only those would be able to go who have the
money to get tickets; many are too poor to go." Allan J. Mc-
Laughlin, the surgeon in charge of the United States Public Health
Station at Naples, stated in an interview with the chairman of the
Immigration Commission: "I think that it is true that the United
States gets the cream of those who have enterprise enough to
exercise an initiative. In fact, one of the complaints of the present
day of the Italian officials is that the very best young blood of the
Italian plebes is going out of the country. They recognize that fact.
It is the man with the initiative who leaves."[21]

Emigrants from Italy and elsewhere in Southern and Eastern
Europe benefited from the introduction in the late nineteenth century of the steamship for transatlantic travel. In fact, without the
steamship it would have been almost impossible for most Southern
and Eastern-European emigrants to have made the voyage to the
United States. Previously the Atlantic crossing had taken a month
or more by sailing ship from a British, French, or German port,
and was a perilous experience. By steamship the same trip could
be made in ten days to two weeks and was safer and far more
comfortable than it had previously been. Furthermore, in the
steamship era it was possible to travel from a port on the Mediterranean instead of having to journey overland to leave from a
Northern European port.

Naples, Palermo, Messina, and Genoa were the Italian ports of
embarkation for emigrants leaving for overseas destinations. After
fhe turn of the century Naples emerged, according to the United
States Immigration Commission, as the leading European port "in
the number of emigrants embarking for America."[22] Between
twelve and fourteen steamship companies at various times offered
direct service between Naples and New York City. The major

European lines operated out of Naples, including White Star,
North German Lloyd, Navigazione Generale Italiana, Fabre,
Lloyd-Italiano, and Hamburg-American.

Even with the improvements that the steamship brought the
crossing was not a pleasant or enjoyable experience. Most of the
peasants had never strayed far from their home village much less
been on an ocean voyage. The trip itself from an Italian port
through the Mediterranean and across the Atlantic usually took
two to three weeks. For the emigrants, who traveled steerage, the
voyage was harrowing. The quarters were overcrowded and badly
ventilated, and there was limited access to deck space. Conditions
were even worse during bad weather, which was a frequent occur-
rence on the turbulent Atlantic. The passage across the ocean
"seemed to have been so calculated," one emigrant recalled, "as to
inflict upon us the last, full measure of suffering and indignity, and
to impress upon us for the last time that we were the 'wretched
refuse' of the earth; to exact from us a final price for the privileges
we hoped to enjoy in America."[23]

In 1903 an American writer, Broughton Brandenburg, and his
wife undertook an assignment from *Leslie's Monthly* to imper-
sonate Italian emigrants and travel in steerage of a passenger ship
from Naples to New York. The project resulted in a well-received
book, *Imported Americans*. The Brandenburgs studied the Italian
language and then moved into an imigrant neighborhood in New
York. When "duly prepared and informed" they went to Europe
"with some of the returning Italians" and after studying "the actual
conditions" in the Southern Italian countryside began the journey
back to America. In Naples they boarded a steamship with emigrants from all parts of the Kingdom: "If one looked carefully
there were to be seen twenty different sorts of costumes of the
contadini."[24]

The "motley assemblage" was herded into huge compartments.
All the women, young children, and babies were placed in one
compartment, and the vastly larger numbers of men and older boys
slept in the other compartments. There was serious overcrowding

in all the compartments occupied by emigrants. Beds were double- or triple-tiered affairs with iron frameworks that supported burlap-covered bags of straw, grass, or waste which served as mattresses. As in most ships which depended on the emigrant trade, little thought or effort was devoted to the comfort or welfare of passengers in steerage. Thus few vessels provided enough space for steerage passengers to sit down at a table for their meals. "For such quarters and accommodations as I have described," Brandenburg noted with more than a trace of bitterness, "the emigrant pays half the sum that would buy a first-class passage. A comparison of the two classes shows where the steamship company makes the most money."[25] Brandenburg was correct in this observation. Although steamship companies lavished attention and services on the occupants of first-class accommodations, it was the masses packed in the steerage that provided the sizable profits made by steamship companies involved in the Atlantic passenger trade in the decades before World War I.

Crew members generally treated steerage passengers with contempt, on those occasions when they acknowledged their existence. Even the most unpleasant of voyages did, however, eventually come to an end and when the ship docked in an American port, usually New York, the weary and often sick passengers were ready to begin their experience as immigrants.

PART II

THE IMMIGRANT ERA

CHAPTER 3

The Immigrant Tide

During the century following the end of the Napoleonic wars in 1815 the United States became a "country of immigrants." Approximately 32 million Europeans came, in the words of Maldwyn Jones, "in a series of gigantic waves, each more powerful than the last and separated one from another only by short periods of time."[1] Newcomers from Ireland, Germany, and elsewhere in Northern and Western Europe—the so-called "old" immigrants—arrived in two great waves during the decades between 1815 and the 1880s.

Five million immigrated in the first wave, which reached its crest in 1854, when 428,000 arrived. During the decades between the Civil War and the 1880s, a second wave of ten million more Northern Europeans arrived. They were followed by the "new" immigrants from Southern and Eastern Europe, approximately seventeen million of whom poured into the country in the thirty-five years before World War I. Italians formed part of this last, and largest, wave of immigrants. In 1914 there were no signs of a slackening but the onset of war in Europe intervened to bring a halt to the Atlantic migration. The flow of immigrants into the United States began again as soon as the war ended but restrictionists who had for decades attempted to slow if not halt further immigration finally gained public support and had their way.

Italian immigration, rather than resembling a series of waves of increasing size could be depicted as two trickles and a tidal wave. In the years before 1880 the number of newcomers was, as Robert F. Foerster has noted, very small: "Records for the United States began in 1820 when 30 Italians arrived. There were less than 75 a year until 1833; less than 2000 until 1870 when 2,891 arrived. The year 1873 brought 8,757, a number not again reached until 1880 when 12,354 arrived."[2]

Between 1820 and 1860 (official immigration statistics were not kept until 1820) fewer than 14,000 Italians arrived in the United States, nearly three-quarters during the decade of the fifties. These early arrivals, most of whom intended their settlement in America to be permanent, generally came from Italy's Northern provinces. Many were educated persons or skilled workers, among them teachers, entertainers—including actors, musicians, and ballet dancers—stonecutters, and other craftsmen. There was also a sprinkling of political and religious refugees.

By 1860 Italians were to be found in every state in the Union, despite the limited size of the immigration. In 1860 the largest number of Italians resided in California (2,805), New York (1,862), and Louisiana (1,134). The attraction of Louisiana and California continued into the following years. As late as 1890 Italians were more numerous in the Pacific states than they were in New England. In that year California contained 15,495 Italians. Louisiana, with 7,767 immigrants, was beginning to lose its appeal as Italians found greater economic opportunity elsewhere. The effects of the so-called New Orleans Incident of 1890–91 further decreased the attraction of the Bayou State. On October 15, 1890, the New Orleans police chief, David Hennessy, was murdered. The press and the public assumed that Italians were responsible but a jury found the accused innocent. The verdict sent the concerned citizens of the city into a fury. On March 14, 1891, a mob stormed the parish prison and lynched and systematically shot or clubbed to death every Italian they found—eleven at final count. This was but one of at least seven lynchings of Italians in Louisiana, Mississippi, North Carolina, and elsewhere in the South in the two decades after 1890. The immigrants recognized, for reasons to be discussed below, that they were not welcome and went elsewhere.

As the tide from Southern Italy swelled in the period after 1890

Table 3. Italian Immigration to the United States, 1820–1920

Years	Number of Immigrants
1820–1830	439
1831–1840	2,253
1841–1850	1,870
1851–1860	9,231
1861–1870	11,725
1871–1880	55,759
1881–1890	307,309
1891–1900	651,893
1901–1910	2,045,877
1911–1920	1,109,524
Total	4,205,880

Based on U.S. Bureau of the Census, *Historical Statistics of the United States: Colonial Times to 1970*, Part 1, pp. 105–6.

the destination increasingly became the urban-industrial states of the East and Middle West. The majority of the immigrants settled in the Middle-Atlantic states of New York, New Jersey, and Pennsylvania, in New England, and such Middle-Western states as Ohio and Illinois.

While many went into agriculture, most, even in the early decades of the immigration, settled in cities where they felt greater economic opportunity existed. A contrast also began to emerge between the experience of immigrants in the cities of the East and those who settled in the West.

In the two decades from 1860 to 1880 nearly 68,000 Italians arrived. Although most still came from the North the source was beginning to shift to Southern Italy. Peasants and farm laborers entered the country in increasing numbers, many remaining only a few months or years before returning to Italy. During these decades Italian colonies in New York, Chicago, New Orleans, San

Francisco, and other cities began to take definite shape, and such institutions as the press, mutual-aid societies, and the padrone system began to function.

By 1880, according to Foerster, "the formative years of Italian immigration may be said to have been completed."[3] In 1880 fewer than 45,000 Italians lived in the the United States. Nearly one million Italians arrived during the following twenty years. The flood of Italian immigration reached its height after the turn of the century, and before it began to ebb in the early 1920s another three and a half million had come.

In the years between 1880 and World War I approximmately 80 percent of Italian immigrants were from Southern provinces. During this period the immigration was characterized by a heavy preponderance of unskilled working-age males. Thus of the 2,250,000 Italians who arrived between 1899 and 1910 males comprised more than three-quarters of the total, and of the males nearly 85 percent were between the ages of fourteen and forty-five. The occupational background of these men and boys in agricultural labor in Italy qualified them only for jobs as unskilled laborers in an America which was rapidly becoming an urbanized and highly industrialized nation.

With few exceptions the immigrants flocked to America for economic reasons, as Stefano Miele, a turn-of-the-century arrival, freely acknowledged:

If I am to be frank, then I shall say that I left Italy and came to America for the sole purpose of making money. Neither the laws of Italy nor the laws of America, neither the government of the one nor the government of the other, influenced me in any way. I suffered no political oppression in Italy. I was not seeking political ideals: as a matter of fact, I was quite satisfied with those of my native land. If I could have worked my way up in my chosen profession in Italy, I would have stayed in Italy. But repeated efforts showed me that I could not. America was the land of opportunity, and so I came, intending to make money and then return to Italy. This is true of most Italian emigrants to America.[4]

Unlike "most Italian emigrants," however, Miele became a very successful professional man, a lawyer, in his adopted homeland.

One of the major characteristics of the Italian immigration to the United States was its seasonal nature. As one observer in 1906 noted: "They form a stream of workers that ebbs and flows from Italy to America in instant response to demand."[5] Southern Italians were, in this view, "the most mobile supply of labor that this country has ever known." Eight years earlier, the New York Bureau of Labor Statistics, in its *Annual Report* for 1898, in a rather convoluted prose observed that Italians "who go to work in the United States, who leave their families in Italy, who send to them all their earnings, nearly, and who are in the United States only temporarily for the purpose of making money with the ultimate design of returning to Italy, is very great."[6]

A very large proportion of the immigration was composed of migratory laborers who came here to work on construction or other seasonal jobs for eight or nine months of the year and then returned to spend the winter in Italy. Others left the United States during the winter months to work as agricultural laborers in Latin America. The seasons in South America are the reverse of those in the United States and Europe, and Italians stayed in the Southern Hemisphere from November to March. The best economic opportunities were in Argentina and Brazil and that is where most of the immigrants went. There, according to a contemporary, Italian immigrants "are not navvies or agricultural laborers; the richest merchants, the biggest contractors and stock-brokers, the most successful barristers, doctors, engineers and other professional men are Italians."[7]

In the huge Brazilian state of Rio, "with an area nearly as large as Europe and of boundless fertility," the chief building firm, the largest flour mills belonged to Italians while "the banks, the hat industry, the textile manufacturers [were] largely in their hands." In Argentina, Italians enjoyed even greater success. "Italian architects and masons . . . built the greater part of Buenos Aires and La Plata." In addition, they owned "nearly half the commercial firms of Buenos Aires, with a capital of $150,000,000, and more than half its workshops."[8] Eventually, a recent historian has shown, Italians came to play a decisive role in the Argentine economy which "at the time, was one of the fastest growing in the world. They were the largest single group of owners and workers of industrial and commercial establishments."[9]

Because of their migratory ways the immigrant laborers in the United States came to be known as "birds of passage." (In Latin America similar designations were employed. Argentinians, for example, referred to Italian laborers as *golondrinas*, or swallows.) Eventually most of the immigrants settled in the New World but in numerous instances the voyages back and forth to Italy, Latin America, or elsewhere, were repeated several times.

Some contemporaries noted that after 1900 the return migration to Italy was especially heavy during bad economic periods in the United States. Writing in 1912 Cyrus Sulzberger concluded that "the so-called bird of passage instead of being a menace to our industrial conditions, is their greatest help. He gives flexibility: comes when there is a demand for his work and departs when the demand is over."[10] Thus in the depression year of 1904 more than 134,000 Italian immigrants returned to Europe. The reverse migration, in effect, served as a safety valve for depressed industrial towns and cities in the United States.

The laborers who returned to Europe during hard times were not, according to research conducted by W. B. Bailey of Yale University, "the ones who have saved the most money and made the greatest advance in this country." Instead it was the less successful workers who departed from the United States during depression years. Bailey observed that during the depression of 1907–8 "nearly three thousand Italians left New Haven, Connecticut for the home country, and a careful investigation showed that those to depart were the ones who felt themselves in the poorest position to withstand a period of depression." The result of such return migration during times of economic crisis was to limit the decline in wages and "to free the community from the necessity of supporting a number of unemployed who have made scant provision for the future." Bailey concluded that wages were prevented from falling lower than they did in industrial depressions like the one in 1907–8 in part because of "the reduction in the supply of labor caused by the withdrawal over-sea of so many thousands of temporary migrants."[11]

In the mid-1920s University of Wisconsin economics professor Harry Jerome conducted exhaustive research under the auspices of the National Bureau of Economic Research to determine the relationship between the migration and American business cycles in the century between 1815 and 1914. In a richly statistical study he confirmed the findings of earlier scholars. "There is a close relationship," Jerome concluded, "between the cyclical oscillations of employment and those of immigration and emigration, and a moderately close resemblance in the respective seasonal fluctuations, with considerable reason to believe that this similarity, particularly in the cyclical oscillations, is due to a sensitiveness of migration to employment conditions."[12]

Despite the departure of less-successful workers during depression years Italian immigration after the turn of the century became more stable as women and children joined the men who came seeking their fortunes. As early as 1901 the United States Industrial Commission recognized that after a few years of travel back and forth to Europe or Latin America either the family was brought over or, if the man was single, it was observed, he "marries and settles down here, becoming a permanent member of the community."[13]

The arrival of Southern-Italian family units in the period after 1900 was the last link in a migratory chain that began in the 1870s and 1880s with the efforts of padrones to supply labor for American employers. Padrones, or labor agents, generally recruited unskilled Southern Italians for railroad or other construction or maintenance work. Although the padrone system played a key role in the early stages of the immigration, once the movement was firmly under way the services provided by labor agents were no longer necessary and the system declined in importance.

As the early immigrants became acquainted with American conditions and practices they were better able to look after themselves and also to help later arrivals. During this intermediate stage in the migration process individual male workers assisted male relatives and friends of working age to emigrate. "New arrivals usually went directly to the relatives and friends who had financed their passage, and relied on them to find their first lodgings and employment."[14] This was not an organized process but involved a series of individual decisions and actions. Nevertheless it accounted for a large proportion of the male immigration from Southern Italy.

The final stage came when adult male immigrants concluded that it was no longer advantageous, economically or otherwise, to continue the periodic travel overseas and sent for wives and children. Not only was money saved by not traveling back and forth to Italy, but because wives and children were brought to the United States and put to work the family income was increased. Some of the immigrants who settled down in the New World did not, however, send for the families left behind in Italy. In fact, they apparently had no intention of sending for wives and children. They simply broke off all contact and, without bothering to obtain divorces from Old World spouses, married again and started new families here in America. This manner of "closing" the "chain of migration" was, according to Richard Juliani, "a rather ordinary experience for many Italians."[15]

Despite the arrival of increasing numbers of family units in the years after 1900 the "bird of passage" aspect of the Southern-Italian immigration did not disappear. Although only 31 percent of the immigrants during the period 1897–1901 and 38 percent during 1902–6 returned to Italy, the repatriation figure grew to an incredible 72.6 percent during the next five-year period, which included the years 1907 and 1908, a time of severe industrial crisis in America.

An estimated 97 percent of Italians coming to the United States landed in New York City. From there they fanned out through the country although the majority remained close to the port of arrival or settled in urban-industrial centers of the Middle West. Of a total 2,284,601 Italians who came to the United States between 1899 and 1910, approximately three-quarters went to the heavily urbanized states of New York (993,113), Pennsylvania (429,200), Massachusetts (154,882), and New Jersey (118,680). Another 111,249 were attracted to Illinois and 58,699 to Ohio, largely because of the economic opportunities available in the cities of Chicago and Cleveland. Northern Italians were still drawn across the country to California and particularly to the city of San Francisco, which in 1910 contained 16,918 Italian immigrants.

The concentration of Italians in the slum areas of large cities and in low-paying occupations was a source of deep concern to contemporary observers. They sincerely believed that urban difficulties could be alleviated by encouraging immigrants to move to rural areas. Because most of the newcomers had engaged in farm labor in Italy, it seemed logical that they would hope to settle on farms in America.

Contemporaries were convinced that Italians would become Americanized more rapidly in a rural setting than they would in a city. If only immigrants would go to farms instead of crowding into the slums of large cities, the Commissioner-General of Immigration Frank P. Sargent maintained in 1904, "there would be no need to fear for the future."[16] In 1907 economist John R. Commons expressed a similar concern. In contrast to Italians who "in the immigrant stage . . . are helpless," Germans, Scandinavians and other earlier immigrant groups from Northern Europe had been from the start "the model farmers of America" because of their "thrift, self-reliance, and intense agriculture." He added, "the least self-reliant or forehanded, like the . . . Italians, seek the cities in greater proportions than those sturdy races like the Scandinavians, English, Scotch and Germans."[17] As late as 1921 Peter A. Speek, in a volume on immigrants in agriculture for the *Americanization Studies* series, could claim that "some seemingly insurmountable reason prevented them [Italians and other "new" immigrants] from following their desires and calling" by settling on the land.[18]

To promote the movement of Italians to farms, the Italian and United States governments, individual states, and even private agencies supported the establishment of agricultural colonies throughout the country, and especially in Texas, Arkansas, Mississippi, Louisiana, and Alabama. Italian-American leaders also shared this view. In testimony before the United States Industrial Commission in 1901 Alessandro Mastro-Valerio, editor of Chicago's *La Tribuna Italiana Transatlantica,* reinforced the belief of Americans that Italian immigrants wanted desperately to go into agriculture but did not know "how to get the land and the means to work it until it produces." As a result, he said, they found themselves bottled up in cities. This was not right, Mastro-Valerio believed. Because most of the immigrants had engaged in farm labor in Italy it seemed logical to him that they would want to settle on the land in America. They were "country people, therefore they should have been established in the country."[19] His view was that Americans had a responsibility for getting the immigrants out of the urban slums and into agriculture. Another leader maintained in an article published in 1905 that "the means best adapted to solving this problem [getting the immigrants out of the cities] would appear to be the formation of colonizing societies which should propose to found agricultural colonies composed of Italian peasants."[20]

Despite auspicious beginnings and official support, most of the rural ventures undertaken ended in failure. One visitor to an early farming settlement noted not only poorly constructed houses with few weatherproof features, where "members of the colony sleep together without distinction as to age or sex," but also a total lack of sanitation facilities and a financial organization structured in such a way as to keep the colonists perpetually in debt.[21]

Distasteful as these conditions appear now, their impact on the immigrants was slight. Such factors as ignorance of opportunity, unfamiliar climate, squalid living conditions, and cost of land did not deter colonists who wanted to farm. A more important factor caused immigrant unwillingness to settle in rural areas in the United States; most Southern Italians simply did not emigrate to North America, or to Latin America for that matter, with hopes or intentions of farming. Like the majority of members of all the "new" immigrant groups to this country, they arrived seeking economic opportunity. In the United States and Latin America, urban areas offered these opportunities, agriculture did not.

In countries that offered opportunities in agriculture, however, immigrants went into agriculture, as in North Africa. Southern Italians, and especially Sicilians, comprised 95 percent of the Italian immigration to North Africa and of that total fully 80 percent engaged in agriculture. Thus, in his definitive history of modern Sicily, Denis Mack Smith noted that by 1900 Sicilians "had achieved in Tunisia under French rule the peasant proprietorship which was so elusive at home." In the process they also "had exploded a whole series of myths by proving that they would take easily to radical agricultural innovations and could create flourishing farms out of conditions not unlike those on the *latifondi* [large landed estates] at home."[22]

According to the 1900 Federal census only 6.2 percent of the Italian immigrants in the United States worked on farms. By contrast, in the decades before 1900 approximately two-thirds of the Italian immigrants in Argentina went into agriculture. There they overcame obstacles similar to those in the United States and farmed to great advantage, adapting without difficulty to new crops, soils, markets, and living conditions. It should be noted that most of these immigrants were from Northern Italy and that Southerners, who predominated in the immigration after the 1890s, settled in cities and for reasons similar to those that motivated Southern Italians in the United States to locate in urban areas.

In the last years of the nineteenth and into the twentieth century prospects of financial gain in the United States existed not in agriculture, but in the large urban centers of the East and Middle West. In 1909 Alberto Pecorini recognized this in an article he published in the *Annals*. Italian immigrants poured in "just when the crying need of this country was for mill workers and unskilled laborers of every kind for the building industries. No wonder," Pecorini concluded, "that the Italians crowded into the large cities of the northeast and were chiefly employed in manufactures, just as forty years ago the crying need of the country being for more agricultural workers the immigrants from northwestern Europe went to the West and settled there."[23] The economic realities of contemporary American life were, more than any other factor, primarily responsible for the failure of agricultural colonies founded by Southern Italian immigrants.

The United States Industrial Commission recognized the newcomers' desire for economic betterment in its summary volume, published in 1902, in which it examined the factors responsible for immigrant concentration in cities. The Commission noted first "the general movement of all modern industrial peoples toward urban life—a movement quite characteristic of the American people themselves." For the foreign-born, additional factors reinforced this trend: the isolation of farm life in the United States, in contrast to agricultural areas in Europe; immigrant memories of the "hardships and oppression of rural life from which they are struggling to escape"; and ready employment in cities directly upon arrival, generally for higher wages than those paid to farm laborers.[24]

Immigrant difficulties in America stemmed from the cultural problem of adjusting to new living patterns, the result of moving from a rural to an urban environment. Contrary to the commonly held beliefs of the time, assimilation slows or halts in a rural environment, where the community is forced in upon itself by the

lack of outside contacts, and where local customs can be preserved
almost intact. In cities, on the other hand, the intermingling of
peoples and the impact of outside influences that encourage the assimilation process are inevitable. Americans who moved from
farms to cities encountered many of the same problems faced by
Italian immigrants. Numerous adjustments were necessary for
Southern-Italian villagers who migrated to a city in Northern Italy
or to some other European city as well as for those who traveled
across the Atlantic. No matter where they settled the migrants
found themselves in a new and substantially different environment
from that of the rural areas from which they came.

Those Italians who were attracted to farming engaged in different types of agriculture according to the sections of the country in
which they lived. Many Italians living in the large cities of the East
and Middle West learned that it was profitable to raise vegetables
and poultry on the outskirts of town or on a vacant lot in the city.
This activity, truck farming (or market gardening), was particularly attractive to Italians living in New Jersey, Pennsylvania, New
York, Massachusetts, Connecticut, Wisconsin, and Illinois. These
immigrants took over farms abandoned by native Americans who
moved west or switched occupations and moved into the city.
Many truck farmers worked as temporary labor in the city during
the winter season and grew crops in the summer months. Truck
farming was attractive for three reasons: it did not require a large
and long-term investment, it offered immediate returns, and since
farms were generally small in size the immigrant could live near
friends and relatives.

In the South and Southwest, Italians formed numerous colonies
to cultivate cotton, sugar cane, and tobacco. Others produced fruit
and vegetables. Some of these extensive farming ventures were
successful, such as the Sicilian colony located at Bryan, Texas, and
the community at Tontitown, Arkansas. The colony at Bryan was
founded around 1880 by a small group of Sicilian immigrants who
had been hired to do construction work on the main line of the
Houston and Texas Railroad. When the work was finished the

Sicilians remained and bought land along the Brazos River which at the time was quite cheap because the area was regularly flooded. After establishing a more effective system of flood control the immigrants successfully raised cotton, corn, and other crops. Living on farms that varied in size from one hundred to four hundred acres, most of which were family owned, they had developed, by 1909, a "prosperous, happy and law-abiding" community of 3000 people in approximately 500 Sicilian families.[25]

The successful colony at Tontitown was one of the few beneficial results of an experiment launched by New York businessman Austin Corbin in the early 1890s. Corbin conceived the idea of establishing Italian-immigrant farming communities in Arkansas. The first settlement was on a large tract of land at Sunnyside. Unfortunately Corbin died and his heirs withdrew support from the enterprise which was acknowledged "a complete and disastrous failure." The parish priest, Father Pietro Bandini, refused to admit failure or to abandon "the forlorn remnant" of the Sunnyside colony. Bandini found a good tract of land, borrowed nine hundred dollars to buy equipment, and moved the ill and nearly penniless survivors of Sunnyside to the new location which he named in honor of Enrico Tonti, La Salle's lieutenant who had established a military post near the Arkansas River. Bandini proved to be a very effective leader. Tontitown was soon acknowledged as "a model Italian colony."[26]

By 1912 Tontitown was a flourishing community of 700 inhabitants who owned 4,760 acres of productive farm land, the value of which increased from the original $15 per acre to between $50 and $150 per acre. Every family owned its own home, land, and livestock. The people cultivated vineyards and grew bumper crops of a variety of fruit and vegetables, including apples, strawberries, peaches, onions, peas, and beans. The village contained "a modern hotel," a town hall, three stores, a post office, a church, and a school, as well as a broom factory, a brickyard, a blacksmith shop, a cobbler's shop, and three creameries for the production of butter and cheese. Tontitown appeared to be "a new hope for our newest citizens and for the small seekers for land."[27] Unfortunately, the hope was not borne out elsewhere. Despite a few glittering successes most agricultural colonies ended in failure. These failures were generally due to weak and inconsistent leadership, unpleasant living conditions, poor farming land, and the race issue.

American Southerners viewed Italian farmers as a replacement for black tenant farmers. One Louisiana cotton-plantation owner who employed Italian labor for the first time in 1906 stated that "now that the harvest is over I am prepared to say that the Italians I worked on my place the past season gave entire satisfaction. Although they are totally unfamiliar with cotton-raising methods, they got better results than did any other [that is, black] labor."[28]

Generally Italians became dissatisfied with the economic arrangements favored by the native community and demanded better financial conditions and more desirable land. More importantly, the newly arrived immigrants did not understand or adhere to traditional class and racial arrangements. A tendency on the part of Italians in various parts of the South to mingle socially with black neighbors offended the sensibilities of whites, while their political cooperation in the 1890s in the Populist Party was a threat to white solidarity. The economic interests and needs of Italian immigrants in the South, as historian George E. Cunningham has noted, fitted the philosophy of the Populists more than they did the Democrats, the dominant political party and a major bulwark of "white supremacy" in the South. Whites attempted to deal with the situation with lynchings and public whippings. All of these factors played a part in the decision by most Italians to look outside the South for opportunity. Those who remained learned they had better adopt the customs, attitudes, and prejudices of white Southerners, and just as soon as they possibly could. Bitter experience taught Italians that in order to survive they must, in Cunningham's words, "look with loathing upon everything that the native whites loathed. Once they did so, the Italians could gain acceptance among the native whites, though not at first on a basis of complete equality."[29]

Most of the Italian settlements in the western parts of the United States were located in California although colonies also existed near Portland, Oregon, Tacoma and Seattle, Washington, and Denver, Colorado. The majority of the farmers began as tenants but later bought the land they cultivated, often through partnerships. They worked as dairy farmers or grew fruit or vegetables. In the Tacoma area Italians operated a very successful cut-flower cooperative. Generally the land was not owned by individuals or even by families, but by the group. Although Southern Italians predominated in farming ventures east of the Rocky Mountains, Northern Italians dominated agriculture on the West Coast. They achieved great financial success from vine growing and wine making in the California counties of Sonoma, Mendocino, Napa, Fresno, and Madera. In the lands bordering the San Joaquin and Sacramento rivers they grew vegetables while truck farming was popular in settlements located near large cities.

Italian truck gardeners in the San Francisco Bay Area raised acres and acres of lettuce, spinach, cabbages, artichokes, bell peppers, eggplant, and strawberries. Farms stretched over the hills and the sand dunes of the area. Every piece of available land in the peninsula was placed under cultivation. Italians worked long and hard and reaped financial rewards for the high productivity of their farms. In 1910 Italian truck farms in the Bay Area produced crops valued at approximately nineteen million dollars. An important outgrowth of Bay Area agriculture was the development of the canning industry. One of the pioneers of that industry was Marco J. Fontana, a native of Genoa, who, in 1891, founded M. J. Fontana and Company. In 1899 he was instrumental in the formation of the California Fruit Canners' Association. Formed with a capital outlay of three and a half million dollars the company "soon controlled a great part of the California canning industry."[30] Fontana originated the brand name Marca del Monte, which was shortened to the well-known Del Monte. Later the Fontana cannery became part of the vast holdings of the California Packing Corporation. Calpac, as it is known, has become the largest fruit-

and-vegetable canning organization in the world, with annual sales in excess of five hundred million dollars.

Other Italians turned to seasonal farm labor, usually during the months from April or May to October. In the East, workers left their city homes in the spring and followed the berry crops northward. After completing this work they waited for the cranberry crops to ripen in the autumn. In Wisconsin, Italians competed with Poles to harvest cranberries and beets. The major attraction of seasonal agricultural labor was that it required little skill or strength and hence could be done by entire families, wives and children included. It provided a useful and financially rewarding adjunct for Italian (and other new immigrant) workers who also held industrial jobs, generally in nearby cities.

Despite prodigious and continuous efforts to encourage immigrants to settle in rural areas, the central focus of the Italian-American experience was on the cities and not the nation's rural areas. Clearly, new arrivals faced the basic problem not of escaping from a mythical urban "trap" or of finding agricultural jobs, but rather of settling into their new ways of life, that of the urban immigrant community.

CHAPTER 4

Italian Immigrants in Urban America

The pattern of settlement in the large industrial centers of the East and Middle West began with the founding of the immigrant community by Northern Italians, who tended to predominate until the 1880s. The original enclave started in or near the central city—that is, the business area—and was characterized by the movement of economically successful newcomers out of the slum-area ethnic district into the wider American community. Newcomers from overseas swarmed into the colony, filling vacancies and creating or contributing to problems in overcrowded and rapidly deteriorating neighborhoods.

Slum dwellers, sociologist John Seeley has shown, react in different ways to the environment in which they find themselves. Some believe they are in the slum to stay while others feel they are there only temporarily. The adaptation of the first group consists of passive acceptance "of the nearly unfit-for-human-habitation shacks and shanties, holes and cellars of the area—provided only they be available at 'that low rent.'" These are what Seeley has labeled the " '*adjusted poor.*' " In contrast the " '*respectable poor*' " are in the slum because of necessity. Although they are generally as badly off financially as the "adjusted poor" they do not willingly accept their condition. "These people are unadjusted or unreconciled to the slum in the sense that all their values and identifications and most of their associations are outside it." These upwardly mobile members of the lower class "pay their bills, mind their own business, remain well within the law, hold the aspirations and, within their means, practice the lifeways of a socially

higher class, most of whose members far outrank them economically."[1] This is an apt characterization of the aspirations and
actions of most Italian immigrants, as Antonio Stella has demonstrated. Stella, a physician who worked among Italians in New
York City in the period before World War I, acknowledged that
Italian immigrants "reside in the poorest quarters and in the slums,
so-called, not because they like to be there," but because necessity
required it. "They have nothing, in fact, in common with the slum
population proper, nor do they bring or contribute any of the
degrading characteristics of the professional vagrant or tramp
which [sic] we meet among the 'people of the abyss.' " Stella also
recognized that one of the compelling reasons for immigrants to
locate in a slum neighborhood was that "their work is there."[2]

For new urban dwellers, housing had to meet two essential conditions: it must be cheap, and it must be within walking distance
of work. Central-city neighborhoods provided ideal locations, and
all available structures—warehouses and stables as well as single-
family detached houses—were converted into multifamily, low-
rent dwellings. These buildings returned handsome profits to owners because of their heavy population densities; little, if any,
money went into improving structures or facilities. New construction took the form of tenement housing, designed to concentrate as
many people as possible into a limited amount of space.

Living conditions in urban immigrant neighborhoods were indeed abominable. The Italian colony on New York's Lower East
Side was in 1893 described as "probably one of the most filthy
localities in the city. Here, surrounded by tall brick tenements and
frame rookeries, amid the sickening odors of decaying vegetable
matter and filth, the streets crowded with swarthy men, women
and children, dirty but picturesque withal—here can be found the
home of the Italian." In the tenements "families upon families"
were "huddled together, living, eating and sleeping in one room;
indeed, in many cases a room barely 8 × 10 feet will hold as many
as ten persons." American observers concluded that the immigrants were attracted to such unpleasant living conditions. The

Italian "seems to thrive on dirt and, as a consequence, is not in the least troubled by it."[3]

The largest and most congested immigrant areas were in New York. Walk-up tenements rose to five and six stories and occupied all the property except for a narrow strip at the rear of the lot. In most other cities, tenements generally had two or three stories, but an additional hazard in the form of the rear tenement threatened the welfare of the inhabitants. In order to provide cramped living space for even more tenants, property owners tacked one or more flimsy structures onto the back of larger tenement buildings. The congested rear tenements of Chicago, St. Louis, and Philadelphia were as destructive to the health and lives of the residents as were New York's multistory firetraps.

Core-area neighborhoods, which prior to the mid-nineteenth century had been upper- and middle-income communities, quickly turned into unsightly, overcrowded slums. The original residents departed for new homes on the periphery and in the suburbs "because of the threatened encroachment of commercial activities" and an invading horde of immigrants.[4] The inner-city slums exhibited social disorganization and personal degradation, poverty and pauperism, crime and corruption. Contemporaries feared for the future of their cities and indeed, for the nation itself. A report prepared in 1857 commented on tenement-area conditions in New York City:

These immigrants . . . are destitute, sick, ignorant, abject. They demand immediate food, garb, shelter, and not only immediate but permanent means of obtaining these necessities. . . . The men of families or feeble widows with three or four children, are forced to remain in the neighborhood of the landing place, because absolutely unable to move away from it. . . . They swarm in filthy localities, engendering disease, and enduring every species of suffering. . . . They are often habitual sots, diseased and reckless, living precariously, considering themselves outcasts, and careless of any change in their condition.[5]

This report referred to "old" immigrants, principally Irish and Germans; later reports used similar (sometimes identical) wording to describe conditions among Italians and other "new" immigrant groups before World War I. In 1922 John Palmer Gavit, a reformer who had been a resident of the Chicago Commons Settlement House, which was situated in the middle of an Italian neighborhood on Chicago's West Side, described the repeating pattern: "Each phase of immigration has been 'the new immigration' at its time; each has been viewed with alarm; each has been described as certain to deteriorate the physical quality of our people and destroy the standard of living and of citizenship."[6]

In general, settlement patterns in Chicago typified the Italian experience in urban America. Northern Italians (most of them from Liguria and Tuscany) founded the early colony in the years after 1850 and dominated the rapidly expanding settlement during the following three decades. The early settlers, who intended their stay in Chicago to be permanent, generally came as family units. Most of the men worked at skilled or semiskilled jobs or found employment in service or trade occupations. Some accumulated extensive amounts of property and money. Most, however, were only moderately successful and, like the post-1880 immigrants from Southern Italy, added to family incomes by sending every available member, including school-age children, out to work.

Chicago's Italian-born population grew from four in 1850 to 100 ten years later. The total increased to 552 in 1870. By the mid-1880s, when the movement from the South began to assume significant proportions, the city contained 4,091 Italians. From that decade until World War I, most new arrivals were Southerners.

Whether from Northern or Southern Italy, newcomers at first settled along the same streets and in the same tenements, and sought jobs where others from their own town or province of origin worked. This early concentration broke down as the immigrants met and mingled with newcomers from other towns and provinces and with non-Italians who lived and worked in close proximity. In the process, they began for the first time to think of themselves as Italians rather than as members of a particular family. Whereas in Southern Italy life centered on family needs and goals, in the

United States the family was neither large enough nor sufficiently influential to insure aid in all emergencies. Instead, in the New World, a community identity and an ethnic consciousness began to evolve, one that differed significantly from the family-dominated society of the Italian South. This sense of community and an awareness of being Italian developed in the United States as a response to changed surroundings.

The community of the immigrant generation served as a staging ground where most newcomers remained until they absorbed new ideas and values that facilitated their adjustment to urban America. It thus fulfilled a vital function both for its inhabitants and for the receiving society by bridging the gap between rural traditions and the city. Italians lived and worked in this community with compatriots from other parts of the Kingdom and also with Irish, Germans, Poles, Scandinavians, and others; many went to church with these "foreigners" and their children attended the same schools. In contrast to the homeland tradition of seeking a spouse from the same place of birth, they began to intermarry with "outsiders" from elsewhere in Italy and even with non-Italians.

Continuing the pattern set by their predecessors from Northern Italy, Southerners whose economic position improved moved away from the colony. If migration from the ethnic settlement—a sign of economic mobility and an indication of a desire for better housing and living conditions—did not take place in the first generation, it generally occurred in the second or third. Contemporary American observers, who did not realize that succeeding waves of newcomers filled the vacancies left by departing immigrants, concluded that Italians, and their children and grandchildren after them, always remained on the same streets and in the same tenements. Americans also assumed that compact, unchanging colonies remained grouped according to place of origin, as indeed existed during the early years of immigration. This cohesion, however, soon broke down. The composition of Italian colonies (like that of other ethnic groups) was in constant flux, with much of the community changing place of residence each year, some to other housing within the colony, others to entirely different areas.

Also contrary to popular belief, Chicago, like other cities, had few blocks and even fewer neighborhoods inhabited exclusively by Italians. Between 1880 and 1920 only limited sections of certain Chicago streets held a 50-percent or higher concentration of Italian immigrants and their children. The population density of Italians in most of the city's various Italian districts fell considerably below 50 percent. Even the Near West Side community in the vicinity of Hull House, which between 1890 and 1920 comprised the largest and most densely concentrated group of Italians in the city, had only a few blocks where Italians constituted 50 to 70 percent of the inhabitants; and they made up only one-third of the area's *total* population. Nevertheless, newspaper reporters, social workers, and the general public characterized this neighborhood, and others like it, as "Italian."

The Near West Side community is still, in the 1980s, universally referred to as being "Italian," largely because even though the Italian element in the population has declined to a minority, churches, restaurants, stores, and other businesses have remained behind to give the area the appearance of ethnic cohesion. Businesses have continued to prosper because in addition to catering to the needs of the dwindling number of residents who remain in the neighborhood, they also serve former residents who have moved to suburbia but return on weekend shopping expeditions. These businesses also attract non-Italians who want to get "authentic" ethnic products or to eat in ethnic restaurants.

Observers of life in Chicago and other cities in the decades before 1920 ignored or did not recognize the gradual shift in the location of Italian districts. Thus the area discussed in one study often differed from that examined in another study, even though the colony in both instances might be labeled "the Near West Side" or "the Near North Side" community. Because the composition of Italian districts underwent rapid and continual change, the miserable, undernourished residents described in one study generally were not the same people examined in subsequent studies.

Italians in Chicago were a group in motion, shifting constantly throughout the city and its nearby suburbs. A 1915 City Department of Public Welfare survey of a West Side Italian community found that nearly half of the district's residents moved every year, some to another dwelling in the same area but many to other parts of the city. Among these were unskilled laborers in search of work or better living conditions. If these goals could not be achieved in Chicago, they went elsewhere in the United States, to a Latin-American city, or back to the home village in Italy.

The New York Italian community was by far the largest in the nation but the immigrant experience in that city largely paralleled that in Chicago and other major cities such as Boston, Baltimore, Philadelphia, Pittsburgh, Cleveland, Detroit, Milwaukee, Kansas City, and Denver.

During the immigration era, 97 percent of the Italians entering the United States landed in New York. Although a large proportion of the immigrants moved on to other destinations, most settled in urban areas, generally large cities. Enough, however, remained

Table 4. Italian Immigrants in Selected American Cities, 1870–1910

	1870	1880	1890	1900	1910
Baltimore	146	358	824	2,042	5,043
Boston	264	1,277	4,718	13,738	31,380
Chicago	552	1,357	5,685	16,008	45,169
New Orleans	1,571	1,995	3,622	5,866	8,066
New York	2,794	12,223	39,951	145,433	340,765
Philadelphia	516	1,656	6,799	17,830	45,308
Pittsburgh	74	248	1,899	5,709	14,120
San Francisco	1,622	2,491	5,212	7,508	16,918

Compiled from population census figures, Ninth through Thirteenth United States Censuses.

Table 5. Percentage of Italian Population
in the Boroughs of New York City, 1900–20

	1900	1910	1920
Manhattan	71.4*	58.6	47.2
Brooklyn	25.6	29.5	35.3
Bronx	*	7.4	10.1
Queens	2.1	3.3	5.1
Richmond	1.1	1.3	2.2
Total Number	145,433	340,765	390,832

* In 1900 Bronx data was listed with Manhattan. The Bronx did not become a separate county until 1904.

Based on Thomas Kessner, *The Golden Door: Italian and Jewish Immigrant Mobility in New York City 1880–1915* (New York, 1977), p. 155. Data from Federal Census for 1900, 1910, and 1920.

in New York for it to have the largest Italian population in the United States. In the years before World War I New York housed more Italians than Florence, Venice, and Genoa combined.

Many of those who could afford to do so moved away from New York and its congested neighborhoods. The result, John Foster Carr noted in 1906, was that "in proportion to its size it is the least prosperous Italian colony in the country, and shelters a considerable part of our immigrant failures—those who cannot fall into step with the march of American life."[7] Nevertheless, statistician Eliot Lord noted in 1905, "the thrift of the [New York] Italian is so exceptional that even bootblacks and common laborers sometimes save enough to figure as tenement landlords." Also in 1905 immigrant group leader Gino Speranza, at the time vice-president of the Society for the Protection of Italian Immigrants, documented the financial assets of Italians in the city. According to Speranza, savings accounts held by Italians totaled more than $15,000,000 while their real estate holdings were valued at $20,000,000. He estimated that Italians owned some 10,000 stores in the city, with a value of $7,000,000. The total material value of property of the New York Italian colony was $60,000,-000, an impressive figure, but one that was proportionately inferior to Italian achievements in such cities as Chicago, San Francisco, and Boston, Speranza admitted. It was nevertheless "a fair showing for the greatest 'dumping ground' of America."[8]

New York Italians also displayed extensive residential mobility. In 1905 settlement-house worker Lillian Betts noted that Italian immigrants she observed in the district below Fourteenth Street stayed "hardly two months . . . in the same rooms" before they moved on. In fact "a residence of one year for a tenant is remarkable."[9]

It is not difficult to understand why Italians were eager to depart from colonies like the one on the Lower East Side. In 1910 over 40,000 people, approximately 95 percent of whom were Italian immigrants and their children, were packed into a seventeen-block area. This was an average population of about 1,417 per block. Mary Frasca, director of the Mulberry Community House, described life on the Lower East Side: "In this section there are only three public schools, two board of health milk stations and a dispensary. There is no public bath [and no baths in the tenement houses], no playground, no social center, and indeed an entire lack of other vital needs."[10]

Historian Thomas Kessner, who studied Italian and Jewish mobility patterns in New York, found that in 1890 while 79 percent of the Italian sample he traced during the decade 1880–90 resided in the heavily congested slum neighborhoods below Fourteenth Street, by 1915 the Italian element in this area had dwindled to 48 percent of the total. This was because by the decade "between 1905 and 1915, residential alternatives expanded and much fewer Italians restricted themselves to the downtown ghettos."[11] By 1915 Italians had not only spread northward across Manhattan Island and into the Bronx, but also eastward into Brooklyn and westward across the Hudson River into Newark and other New Jersey cities.

Italians settled in Brooklyn in increasing numbers after the 1870s, according to Ralph Foster Weld, an authority on the borough's history, in order to "escape overcrowding in Manhattan." Families from Manhattan's densely populated Lower East Side Italian colony crossed the East River in ever-increasing numbers following the opening in 1883 of the Brooklyn Bridge. They first settled along Union and President streets in the vicinity of the waterfront. In the decades before World War I, Weld noted, "Italian colonies spread in all directions—into the Navy Yard district, Gravesend, East New York, Williamsburg, Greenpoint, Ridgewood." Living conditions in these communities were generally deplorable, with "small wooden tenements and crumbling brick dwellings" packed to overflowing with newly arrived immigrants and their families. Some of the structures had been built almost a century before by Yankees and had been handed down from one generation to another and from one immigrant group to the next. "In the Navy Yard district, in Red Hook, Greenpoint, and elsewhere, Old World and New World traditions and ideas were mingled." As time passed and a measure of prosperity came to some of the homes, Antonio or Salvatore or Giuseppe went to college, and came home a sophisticated young American engineer, pharmacist, or lawyer."[12] Instead of settling in the old neighborhood, however, he generally moved to a comfortable suburban community on Long Island or in Westchester County.

The "first large stream" of Italian immigrants, most of them natives of Campania, Calabria, and Sicily, poured into Newark in the 1870s. "Bewildered by the garish, tumultuous life of New York and its teeming 'little Italy,' unhappy and uncomfortable in the sunless, cramped and disease-ridden tenements of New York's slums," Charles Churchill has written, "they set out to find houses more suited to their temperament and background." For increasing numbers of immigrants the answer to the problems posed by tenement life in New York was Newark, "then a comparatively calm and spacious city." Newark, in fact, offered the twin lures of relatively pleasant living conditions and jobs. The city was entering an era of rapid industrial development. An Italian quarter took shape in the neighborhood surrounding Boyden and Drift streets, and as the Italian population in the city rapidly increased, new colonies formed in various parts of Newark's core. In the period between 1870 and 1900 nearly 10,000 immigrants settled in the city. Although the newcomers originally settled in one or another of Newark's Italian districts, dispersal, sooner or later, took place. "It would not have been otherwise," Churchill believes, with "the gradual integration of the Italians with the greater life of Newark, the rise in living standards of the Italian workers, the public school education of their children and the belated but phenomenal growth of an Italian-American business and professional class."[13]

The only communities that developed somewhat differently from the general pattern of Italian urban immigrant settlements were in San Francisco and New Orleans, although the differences were more of degree than of kind. In contrast to other American cities, New Orleans attracted Southern Italians from the beginning of the colony, while the Italian population in San Francisco remained Northern long after other cities were inundated by immigrants from the South. In both cities the Italian communities were wealthier than those in other urban centers, but the patterns of geographical mobility that prevailed elsewhere did so also in San Francisco, and New Orleans.

The first Italians in San Francisco, according to Raymond Dondero, arrived in 1840 when "a Ligurian sea captain named Pietro Bonzi coming by way of Cape Horn reached San Francisco Bay and settled with his brother and son on a 'picturesque height at the northern tip of the San Francisco peninsula' "[14] It is impossible to verify this event but it is certain that Ligurian ships arrived in San Francisco Bay in the early nineteenth century.

In 1848 gold was discovered at a site called Coloma and soon prospectors and miners from all over the world descended upon the Bay Area in the hope of "striking it rich." Although San Franciscans trace their city's origins back to 1776 when the Spanish established a presidio (or fortress) and a mission, around which a town soon grew, in a very real sense San Francisco's history began with the Gold Rush. "From being an utterly unimportant trading and military post it became, within ten years, a thriving port, the clearing house for a vast mining area and something of an international and cosmopolitan metropolis."[15] Between 1848 and 1854 more than two hundred Italians arrived in California to mine for gold. Many of the Italian newcomers had previously settled in Latin America but quickly left when they learned of the gold strike in California. Few found gold but most remained to work as merchants, shopkeepers, truck gardeners, dairy farmers, grape growers, and wine makers. Thus Italians arrived early in the development of the state of California and quickly took their place among the successful members of society.

Federico Biesta, the Kingdom of Sardinia's ranking consular official in San Francisco, reported to the home government in Milan that "the Italian population is one of the best, most active and hardworking in California. Strong, industrious and accustomed to suffering and toil, our nationals tend to their own affairs." Writing in 1857 Biesta noted that "generally, whether in San Francisco or in the interior, the Italians thrive and prosper in their businesses, and there is probably not a village in all California in which Italian business is not well represented."[16]

Most of the Italians who stayed in California settled in or near the state's major city, San Francisco. The San Francisco Italian community, which began to take shape during the 1850s, was formed by disillusioned miners from the Mother Lode country who clustered around the few Italian rooming houses in the city. In the process they formed the nucleus of the city's Italian quarter. By the end of the decade, the first mutual-aid society, the *Società di Mutua Beneficienza*, and the first Italian-language newspaper, *L'Eco Della Patria*, had been started.

Italians, most of them from Liguria, Tuscany, and Piedmont in Northern Italy, settled in the heart of the young but rapidly expanding city. The early immigrants located along Montgomery and a few surrounding streets. As their numbers increased they pushed north across Broadway toward Telegraph Hill, which by the 1870s had become the center of San Francisco's Italian colony. "At the same time that they settled in the heart of the City, Italian immigrants were spreading throughout the City into such districts as Washerwoman's Lagoon, the Hayes Valley, Hunter's Point, throughout the Mission District, Bernal Heights, and beyond the City and County boundary into the neighboring community of Colma and Half Moon Bay."[17]

One of Telegraph Hill's principal attractions was its convenience, being located a fairly short distance from the waterfront as well as the commercial district, the two areas in which most Italians worked. During the following two decades Italians spread out from Telegraph Hill into the North Beach area and then out to Russian Hill. From these neighborhoods economically successful members of the community moved into all parts of the city and its suburbs. Their places in the core-area immigrant districts were taken by new arrivals who, after the turn of the century, came increasingly from Southern Italy. Despite the large influx of Southerners, well over half of San Francisco's Italian immigrant population as late as the 1930s was from Northern Italy.

The experience in New Orleans differed in some respects from that in the urban-industrial North and on the Pacific coast. New Orleans and the state of Louisiana had attracted Sicilians and other Southern Italians long before the great immigrant wave from the Kingdom. Italian immigrants had trickled into the Bayou State during pre-Civil War years, and in 1850 some 915 of them resided there—the largest number to be found in any state of the Union; in contrast, 825 lived in New York, 288 in California, and 196 in Massachusetts.

Immigration followed the long-established citrus-fruit trade from Sicily to New Orleans. The sizable Italian colony in New Orleans in the antebellum period was centered on the fruit trade. "Italians not only imported and distributed the citrus fruit, but they also unloaded the ships and peddled the fruit through the city and surrounding suburbs." In the post-Civil War era Italian immigration to Louisiana continued to follow the already existing citrus trade routes from Sicily. In the late-nineteenth and early-twentieth centuries most of the ships transporting Italian products along with immigrants bound for New Orleans departed from Palermo. Among other examples, in 1880 the British steamship *Scuida* sailed from Palermo to New Orleans with a cargo of lemons and 210 emigrants; in 1887 the steamship *Elysia* transported 613 emigrants and a cargo of lemons and "Mediterranean fruits"; the following year the *Utopia*, with the usual cargo of fruit and "796 Italians from Piana dei Greci, Sicily, sailed from Palermo to New Orleans."[18]

By the 1890s Sicilian immigrants congregated along Ursulines, Chartres, Decatur, Royal, Barracks and other streets in the French Quarter in the vicinity of the waterfront and the French Market in sufficient numbers for the neighborhood to be called "Little Palermo" by other city residents. "Little Palermo" was an area of settlement for new arrivals and for transients who would soon move on to find employment on sugar, cotton, and rice plantations. In November 1905 the Louisiana Immigration Association estimated that ten thousand Italians had passed through New Orleans during the preceding months for destinations in the rural parishes (or counties) of Louisiana. Yet, because of the impact of the Hennessy murder case and the lynchings of 1891, the appeal of New Orleans had already, by 1905, diminished greatly for Italian immigrants to America. The Italians who came were seasonal laborers who made the crossing in the late summer or autumn of each year. They worked on the plantations from September or October to December and after the harvest returned to Italy.

Immigrants who remained in New Orleans, like their counterparts elsewhere, were not confined to any one part of the city. When Italians, like other European immigrants, began to move up the socio-economic ladder, they found it possible to leave their ethnic enclaves if they wished. Obviously the type of discrimination that prevented free residential movement among blacks did not operate among Italians and other white immigrants in New Orleans or in other cities.

At least to 1920 and even later an essential characteristic of Italian settlement in all American cities was that no net or unchanging Italian colony existed. Italian areas of settlement expanded and shifted their location over the years. In addition, individual Southerners, no less than immigrants from Northern provinces, exhibited a high degree of residential mobility. Movement of both colony and individuals generally proceeded outward from the core toward the periphery. The United States Industrial Commission maintained, in 1901, that "the more ambitious and successful" members of New York's Italian community "move to the suburbs and become property owners in Long Island City, Flushing, Corona, Astoria," and other middle- and upper-income towns and hamlets on Long Island.[19] In addition to the movement of individuals to the suburbs, Italian settlements also existed in outer areas of cities and in surrounding working-class suburbs. These "outer" neighborhoods formed during roughly the same years as the settlement of many inner urban communities.

In the Chicago area Italians moved into industrial suburbs at least as early as the 1890s. In the autumn of 1894 Our Lady of Mount Carmel church was established as a mission for the numerous Italian residents of Melrose Park. Nine years later San Rocco opened its doors in Chicago Heights, the first Catholic church in that village. By 1905 religious processions and feasts celebrated at these parishes had become yearly events. In following years Italians continued to pour into Cicero, Melrose Park, Chicago Heights, and other industrial suburbs, where they generally lived in neighborhoods with a sizable Italian element.

In contrast to the industrial suburbs of the East and Middle West, Italian settlements around San Francisco were devoted to truck gardening. During the 1850s a truck-farming community composed largely of Ligurians and Tuscans formed in the Outer Mission District. This was the same decade in which compatriots from the same parts of Italy established San Francisco's major Italian colony in the city's core. Interestingly, while core-area residents moved outward toward suburbia, truck farmers took the first opportunity to move into the core. Raymond Dondero, who examined Italian geographical mobility in San Francisco, found that "whenever a farmer felt sufficiently secure in a financial sense, he would sell or lease his land and move to North Beach." The Mission District and other farming communities declined and eventually disappeared as San Francisco's population increased and pushed out into suburbia. According to Dondero, as the city grew and expanded "new residential areas began to push the truck farms down the peninsula, and the local truck farms were absorbed by extensive housing developments." The old ethnic communities no longer exist, and only an occasional farm house, "conspicuously older than the homes in the adjacent residential development," still stands.[20]

While some Southern Italian immigrants remained permanently in the colony of settlement and even on the same block, the majority quickly moved from the original place of residence and did so frequently thereafter. Whether they were unskilled laborers or had moved up the economic ladder as skilled workers or supervisory personnel in private or public employment, merchants, businessmen, or professionals, Southerners desired and sought better housing and neighborhoods. Discussing the New York experience, Kessner noted that "the conventional picture of stagnant Italians bound to their 'turf' by a strong village-mindedness is not accurate." Kessner also found that "the search for jobs took Italians to work sites across the nation and high repatriation rates carried many back to Europe, undercutting the kind of neighborhood stability that has been taken as a characteristic of Italians."[21]

For members of the immigrant generation, movement generally was from one working-class neighborhood to another, but typically from one located in an undesirable slum area to a pleasanter and less-congested environment. In the decades after 1900 improved and expanded mass-transportation facilities (subways, surface streetcars, and elevated electric lines), accompanied by a decline in transit fares to a nickel, made it possible for laborers as well as members of the middle classes to live beyond walking distance from work. Transportation mobility through public means was important, because for Southern Italians, economic advancement took place largely within the laboring class during the decades of large-scale immigration. Some individuals realized significant financial success, but extensive socio-economic improvement for the group as a whole has come only since the end of immigrant era.

CHAPTER 5

The Economic Adjustment

As with other aspects of the adjustment process, the economic experience of the early-arriving Northern Italians differed from that of the Southerners who came to the United States after 1880. Immigrants from the North typically did not work as common laborers but generally held skilled or semiskilled jobs or found employment in service and trade occupations. Although some possessed considerable wealth, most immigrants from Northern Italy, like the Southerners who came later, had neither financial reserves nor ready cash when they arrived in America. They augmented family incomes by withdrawing children from school and either having them work or charging them with household duties in order to free the mothers for outside jobs.

The Italian government and Italian Americans alike considered the San Francisco Italian community to be the "model colony," with the "most select" and desirable group of urban Italians in the United States. Northern Italians there were successful in banking and small industry; they prospered as fishermen, fish brokers and commission merchants, truck gardeners, viticulturists, horticulturists, and food processors. Next to truck farming the most important industry San Francisco Italians established was commercial fishing. By 1910 Italian fishermen "were providing ninety per cent of all the fish consumed in San Francisco; doing eighty per cent of the commercial fishing in the state; and supplying eighty per cent of the fresh and processed fish shipped out of the state or exported. Some twenty-five hundred Italian fishermen were directly connected with commercial fishing."[1]

The San Francisco Italian colony boasted such business entrepreneurs as Andrea Sbarboro, banker and founder of the Italian-
Swiss Agricultural Colony, a major wine-producing company
under its successor, the Italian Swiss Colony; Marco J. Fontana,
founder of the Marca del Monte canning company, now called Del
Monte; Julio and Ernest Gallo, founders of a company that came
to produce nearly half of all California's wine; Sicilian natives
Joseph and Rosario di Giorgio, whose company became the
world's largest shipper of fresh fruit; and towering above them all
the financial genius, Amadeo Giannini, founder of the Bank of
Italy, later renamed the Bank of America, and the Transamerica
Corporation. The Italian contribution, however, went far beyond
the outstanding accomplishments of these and other highly successful individuals. It was also the "unsung farmers in truck farms
which used to surround the city, the shopkeepers, fishermen,
artisans, and factory workers who worked hard, saved and in-
vested, and helped the city to grow" and who made a major and
lasting contribution "to this center of civilization that we know as
San Francisco."[2]

New York's Italian community also boasted numerous prosperous and productive building contractors, importers, merchants,
manufacturers, bankers and other businessmen, and physicians
and lawyers. On the eve of World War I Frederick Wright, Superintendent of Italian Missions for the Methodist Episcopal Church
in New York City, counted "fifteen hundred or more lawyers, five
hundred physicians, besides a growing number of merchants,
bankers, and businessmen" at work in the city.[3] Others realized
more modest, but still substantial, success through their work in
the building trades, the clothing industry, and as peddlers, vendors,
artisans, bakers, restauranteurs, and confectioners. Some industries, such as the fruit trade, were found by investigators to be "in
the hands of Italians in all its branches, from the Broadway shop
with its inclined plane of glowing color, to the stand at a street
corner."[4] More numerous were those immigrants, even during the
decades when Northern Italians predominated, who, as Howard

Marraro has noted, "lived in a most destitute condition in an unfavorable social milieu, and often in an unhygienic and unwholesome environment."[5] This "unwholesome environment" to which Marraro referred was the Five Points neighborhood on the city's Lower East Side.

As early as the 1850s middle-class American reformers and clergymen expressed deep concern about the miserable conditions of life and labor on the Lower East Side. Of particular concern to them was the welfare of the children. In 1855 the Children's Aid Society of New York City opened an Italian Industrial School in the Five Points neighborhood. During the first ten years of its existence the school trained about five hundred pupils to read and write and attempted to provide them with a trade to help them become self-sufficient adults. The task of aiding the newcomers overwhelmed the resources of reformers as ever-increasing numbers arrived and made New York the principal port of debarkation for Italian immigrants entering the United States.

In Chicago the Northern Italian group consisted largely of settled family units, some containing numerous children. By 1871, according to census data collected by Richard Edwards, the men in this group had become saloon owners and bartenders, vendors and store owners, clerks, barbers and hairdressers, and restaurant owners and employees. Only 18 of the 187 men listed found employment as laborers:

Through hard work and thrift many of the early arrivals became prosperous businessmen who were able to provide a good education for their children and help establish the youngsters in business or the professions. The post-1880 Southern Italian immigrants generally were able to find employment only as common laborers. They appeared to make little economic progress, at least in part because of a steady stream of new arrivals who settled in Italian districts and started at the bottom of the economic ladder. Many immigrants remained unskilled laborers throughout their lives and contributed to the city's economic growth through construction, maintenance, or factory work. Others became affluent merchants,

Table 6. Principal Occupations of Italian-born
Residents of Chicago in 1871

Saloon keeper and bartender	50
Fruit, candy, and ice-cream vendor	27
Confectionery-store owner	25
Clerk	23
Barber and hairdresser	22
Restaurant owner or employee	20
Laborer	18
Tailor	6
Musician	5
Shoemaker	5
Peddler	3
Painter	3

Compiled from Richard Edwards, *Chicago Census Report; and Statistical Review* (Chicago, 1871).

small manufacturers, professionals or businessmen, or qualified for jobs as skilled workmen.

In contrast to the experience elsewhere, Southern Italians composed the majority of both the early and post-1880 arrivals in New Orleans. The city offered many economic opportunities to newcomers, particularly through its importance as a seaport. Although the Irish and blacks monopolized waterfront jobs, a number of Sicilians and other Southern Italians found employment as fishermen, stevedores, and longshoremen. Others became importers, exporters, and retail merchants, and some, fruit-and-vegetable peddlers and dealers. Italian capital and enterprise played a key role in the development of the fruit trade with Latin America, Italy, and elsewhere overseas. Several fortunes were made from this trade. One example was Salvador Oteri, a native of Palermo, Sicily, who by 1891 operated a highly successful wholesale fruit business with a capitalization of half a million dollars and sales throughout the United States of $1,500,000 a year. Oteri employed 250 men in New Orleans, California, Florida, and Latin America in the production, transportation, and distribution of coconuts, oranges, lemons, pineapples, bananas, and various other tropical fruits. He also owned vast plantations in Honduras and a fleet of six large ships to transport the fruit to New Orleans. The Oteri Company was described as "the largest importer in the world of tropical, foreign and domestic fruit and nuts."[6] Oteri was a member of the Chamber of Commerce and the Board of Trade. His son Santo, besides playing a leading role in the operation of the family business, was a director of the Provident Savings, Trust and Safe Deposit Bank, treasurer of the New Orleans Auction and Commission Company, and a member of the real estate firm of Reinach & Co. As a whole the Southern-Italian experience in the Crescent City was highly profitable. By the 1880s the Italians had established themselves as stable, hard-working, and successful residents of New Orleans. This was not the situation in other cities.

During the era of large-scale immigration both journalists and more serious writers generally focused their attention on the employment of Southern Italians as unskilled construction workers. As Edward Steiner, a popular writer of the period observed in 1906, "they are found wherever a shovel of earth needs to be turned or a bed of rock is blasted."[7] This belief stemmed in part from the justly deserved notoriety surrounding the padrone, or labor-boss, system. Overriding attention paid to the boss system had the unfortunate result of obscuring the fact that during the heyday of the padrone, as well as in the period after his decline, Italians engaged in a wide range of economic activities.

Southern-Italian immigrants who flooded into the United States after 1880 generally understood little English, lacked contacts with potential employers in America, and knew nothing about local labor practices. To compensate for these deficiencies they looked for an intermediary—someone who spoke both languages, understood Old World traditions, and had contacts with American employers needing unskilled workers. This intermediary was the labor boss.

Some form of boss system seemed to be typical of non-English-speaking immigrant elements newly arrived in industrial America, including Italians, Greeks, Austrians, Bulgarians, Macedonians, and Mexicans. It was the method by which these groups overcame three immediate problems: language difficulties, financial exigencies, and differences in labor practices. It was, in fact, part of the price that the newcomer had to pay for his strangeness. Dr. Egisto Rossi of the Italian Immigration Bureau summed up the situation: "The padrone system, or bossism, can be defined as the forced tribute which the newly arrived pays to those who are already acquainted with the ways and language of the country."[8]

The Italian padrone system functioned in the United States from the 1860s to the beginning of the twentieth century. Prior to the passage of the Foran Act in 1885, which forbade the importation of immigrant labor under contract, the padrone recruited men in Italy, paid for their transportation, and arranged work for them in the United States, generally in construction. Usually the padrone brought only adult males into the country, but some preferred to recruit entire families, employing the men in manual labor, often forcing the women into prostitution, and sending the children into the streets to shine shoes, play the mouth organ, or steal. After 1885 the padrone acted merely as a private unlicensed labor agent. In fact, most probably acted in this capacity before the mid-1880s as well as after.

Bosses hired men in New York, Chicago, and other cities, and dispatched them to their places of work. The padrone system was best suited to particular kinds of work, especially those demanding a large supply of unskilled labor on short notice and in relatively isolated areas. On rare occasions bosses supplied skilled workers, including masons, carpenters, stonecutters, and machinists.

Because of its role as the principal port of arrival for Italian immigrants, New York City became the center of the padrone system in the United States. It appears that the methods used by bosses in other large cities, except San Francisco, were similar to those practiced in New York. Although San Francisco contained a

large Italian colony, the padrone system did not become an important factor in the city's labor picture. According to an 1897 United
States Department of Labor study of the boss system this difference stemmed from the high cost of transportation across the
country, which served as an effective barrier to a large direct importation, and hence precluded the arrival of the impoverished and
least-fortunate immigrants. The presence of a large and long-set-
tled element of Northern Italians was probably another important
reason for the different labor patterns in San Francisco.

Bosses directed Italian immigrant laborers to most parts of the
United States and even into Canada to build railroads and work at
other construction jobs. Chicago became an important padrone
stronghold, partly because of the city's position as a railroad center
and partly because of its geographical location. Railroad and other
construction jobs tended to be seasonal, and Chicago served as a
clearinghouse for seasonal workers from the entire country.

The padrone (usually of Italian birth or extraction, although
some were Irish or American) met arriving immigrants at the
docks in port cities and at railroad stations in other urban centers
and promised steady work at high wages. Some immigrants did not
succumb to padrone promises at once, but in Italian sections of
any large city stubborn newcomers met with padrone-promoted
pressures and enticements intended to recruit their services for
the boss. Not all immigrants needed to be forced into service for
the boss, however. Many turned toward the padrone because he
offered opportunities to make ready money.

Generally the labor agent negotiated directly with the contractor
and received from him or from representatives of a corporation a
definite order for a specified number of men. In order to obtain
employment through the padrone, immigrants paid a commission
("bossatura") ranging from one to fifteen dollars per man, the size
of the fee depending on such factors as length of employment,
amount of wages, and whether the men were to use padrone facilities.

Not all bosses deliberately made illegal profits, and not all set out to cheat the laborer, but enough did so to give a bad name to the entire group. Many labor agents made use of every available opportunity to overcharge, shortchange, or otherwise take advantage of the men from the moment of hiring to the time of sending them back to the city where they had been hired.

A number of descriptions of padrone camps exist. One, by Domenick Ciolli, an American college student of Italian birth, tells of the living and working conditions in a padrone camp located in Indiana. Ciolli was hired as a common laborer, but because of his education was granted special privileges. The living conditions at this camp were extremely bad. The men lived in windowless railroad cars; boards placed across boxes served as beds. Ciolli found a two-year layer of dirt everywhere. Blankets were covered with vermin, while roaches and bedbugs "held undisputed sway of the beds and their immediate surroundings."[9] All doors were closed at night, effectively keeping out fresh air. The men were not as well protected from rain, which streamed through the porous roof and drenched clothing and bedding. The cars had never been repaired for "they were too old to be used for carrying freight, and were only capable of being used as domiciles for human beings." The only car with windows was the one used by the padrone, the timekeeper (an American who felt contempt for the immigrants), and Ciolli.

The men cooked for themselves, on rusty, perforated tin boxes propped up by stones. The stench was "undefinable," with heaps of rubbish covering the ground, making the outdoors little more bearable than life inside. Supper was the only cooked meal that the men ate. Breakfast consisted of a cup of coffee drunk at three or four in the morning while the men were washing and dressing. Work began at five and continued without interruption until noon. The padrone was quoted as saying: " 'The beasts must not be given a rest. Otherwise they will step over me.' " Lunch consisted of sausages and bread for the younger men and of bread alone for the older workers. Yet with coffee for breakfast, and at best, sausage and bread for lunch, these men worked ten hours a day, seven days a week under all weather conditions.

Despite obviously undesirable characteristics, the labor boss performed a valuable function: he brought together American capital and Italian immigrant labor. Most immigrants lacked education and money, but they had strong arms, a willingness to work, and ambition to earn as much money as possible. What they lacked was an ability to communicate with prospective employers who needed manual laborers. The padrone provided this service for them as well as for employers who usually lacked the means to locate and hire dependable Italian immigrant workers.

In addition to finding jobs, the boss provided other needed services for workers. He collected wages, wrote letters, acted as banker, supplied room and board, and handled dealings between laborers and employers. Unfortunately, too often he abused his trust.

The decade of the 1890s formed a "golden era" for the Italian padrone. Of central importance, however, is that Italian immigration reached its peak in the fourteen years following the turn of the century. It would seem that fortuitous opportunities for unscrupulous labor agents would best present themselves at this time, yet in 1911 the United States Immigration Commission (or Dillingham Commission) found that the boss system could be found "only in a few isolated cases among Italians."[10] The rapid decline of bossism resulted in part from the efforts of social workers and others in the larger outside community concerned about the welfare of immigrants, who pressured state legislatures to pass legislation greatly restricting the power of labor agents.

Along with actions of interested agencies and groups in the American community (which began after 1900), factors of a long-range nature operated within the immigrant colony. The increasingly stable nature of the immigration after the turn of the century helped to reduce the need for the boss. As early as 1897 a report published in the United States Bureau of Labor *Bulletin* pointed out that Italian immigrants had become more settled, a condition indicated by the large numbers who came to the United States to join their immediate families or relations, and were "thus probably to a large extent put out of the reach of the padroni."[11]

The more stable nature of the immigration, increased familiarity with American labor practices and the English language, and the resultant rise in economic status all helped to end the boss system among Italians. By the turn of the century, as the United States Industrial Commission found in its investigations, Italians worked not only at common labor on railroads and other construction and excavation jobs, but also in a variety of trades and professions, and many had become successful merchants, manufacturers, and businessmen. Among these were many whose lives were rags-to-riches success stories. These included Amadeo Obici, the "peanut king"; the Paterno brothers, Charles, Michael, Anthony and Joseph, prominent New York builders and contractors; San Francisco businessman and banker Andrea Sbarboro; and New Orleans hotel owner Antonio Monteleone.

Obici emigrated to the United States in 1889 at the age of eleven from the village of Oderzo in the Venetian hinterland to join an uncle who was in the tailoring business in Scranton, Pennsylvania. After attending school in Scranton for just three months he went to work in a cigar factory. "Brighter prospects soon took him to Wilkes-Barre, where he worked for friends in the fruit-stand business at a salary of $6 a month plus board." He later moved on to other jobs, including that of barkeep, until he made the acquaintance of Mario Peruzzi who worked for a wholesale grocery establishment in Wilkes-Barre and who came from the same part of Italy as Obici. The two young men soon opened a fruit-and-vegetable stand but quickly found that their most popular product was roasted peanuts. In 1906 Obici, as president, and his brother-in-law Peruzzi, who became vice-president and treasurer, incorporated the Planters Nut and Chocolate Company which grew over the decades from a business employing fifteen workers and with a capital stock of $20,000 to a worldwide enterprise doing an annual business of tens of millions of dollars. The short and roundly built Obici who, many people thought, resembled a plump peanut, was an advertising genius and the principal ingredient in his, and Planters', success was imaginative and effective product promotion. Although employing a number of techniques and gimmicks, Obici recognized early the need for a symbol on which to build advertising campaigns as well as to develop a product identity. The symbol chosen and that Planters marketed so effectively was Mr. Peanut, the long-legged, peanut-bodied character with the stovepipe hat and the monocle, which Obici first used in 1916. "Mr. Peanut has since become," *Fortune* Magazine observed in a 1939 profile of Obici and the Planters Company, "one of the most thoroughly publicized personalities in the U.S."[12]

A native of the town of Contessa Entellina in the province of Palermo, Antonio Monteleone arrived in New Orleans in 1870, an impoverished immigrant boy. He began working as apprentice to a shoemaker, later opened his own store, and then started the first shoe factory in the city. By 1890 Monteleone was a shoe manufacturer with $37,000 in taxable property and had become one of the Italian colony's success stories. In the early 1890s he built the Commercial Hotel on Royal and Customhouse (now Iberville) streets. Later he expanded and renamed the building the Monteleone Hotel, which still stands and is one of the famous hostelries in the French Quarter. Monteleone became a director of two banks (the Whitney-Central Bank of New Orleans and the Bank of Hammond, Louisiana, where he owned extensive property) and owner of a brewery.

The four Paterno brothers, Charles, Michael, Anthony, and Joseph, gained great prominence and considerable wealth as builders and contractors in New York City. All four of the Italian natives specialized in the construction of apartment houses, including imposing and ornate structures on Fifth Avenue, Sutton Place, Gracie Square, and West End Avenue. Each brother operated his own business but the brothers cooperated in one venture: they built Casa Italiana at Columbia University.

Northern-Italian-born Andrea Sbarboro, a native of Genoa, was one of San Francisco's most successful Italian-American businessmen from the 1870s until early in the twentieth century. Sbarboro was an early leader in two areas in which Italians realized great success in California: wine making and banking. In the 1870s he organized five savings-and-loan associations to help his fellow Italians save money and, when needed, make available loans to buy homes, start businesses, and purchase farms in the surrounding countryside. In the process Sbarboro "laid the foundation of his fortune." In 1881 he organized the Italian-Swiss Agricultural Association and purchased land in northern Sonoma County near Cloverdale. He named his new vineyard Asti after one of the finest wine-producing regions in Northern Italy's Piedmont. Under the direction of Pietro Rossi, whom Sbarboro hired in 1888 to serve as wine maker, the Italian-Swiss Colony became one of the state's, and the nation's, most successful wine companies. In 1899 Sbarboro opened the doors of the Italian-American Bank, the first commercial bank to be founded by an Italian in the United States.

In his efforts to provide a bank for the "little people" of the Italian community Sbarboro was soon overtaken and then outdone by the financial titan Amadeo P. Giannini, an American-born son of Northern-Italian immigrants. Giannini's Bank of Italy, founded in 1904 with an initial capitalization of $300,000, grew into the world's largest private bank, the Bank of America, with total resources of over $30 billion.

Giannini was one of the most farsighted and innovative bankers of his generation, unlike most bankers of that era, who were cautious and conservative. His bank catered to "the small depositor—the wage earner, the producer, the small businessman, the man who owns a small home or a piece of improved property, the man who is the bone and sinew" of California and the basis for its future progress.[13]

Giannini sought, with great success, to become the banker of the "little people." To reach his public he advertised for new customers, a radical departure from established banking practices of the day, and he introduced branch banking to California and the United States. In the process Giannini competed successfully with the Anglo-Saxon establishment and built a giant institution, the largest bank in the world. His vision was evident in the 1920s when he created a vast holding company which he named Transamerica. Although he later separated the Bank of America from Transamerica, the holding company diversified its portfolio so extensively that it became one of the largest business conglomerates in the United States.

Giannini's bank, from its inception, was not typical of immigrant banking ventures. Immigrant bankers flourished in every part of the United States where newcomers from Southern and Eastern Europe gathered in any considerable numbers. The principal financial transactions of these bankers consisted of receiving deposits and sending money abroad. Most also served as steamship ticket agents, and they often conducted other businesses as well. Hence "banks" could be found in grocery stores, saloons, and other gathering places.

The typical banker had little experience in business methods, ran his office with a minimal accumulation of capital, and for the most part worked outside legal controls. Immigrant bankers were not, for example, restricted as to the kinds of investments they could make with money deposited (restrictions that applied to state and national banks). As a result, speculative ventures of private bankers often ended in disaster, particularly for immigrant depositors; since they had no legal safeguards, they lost their savings. Immigrants who transmitted money to Italy provided bankers with lush opportunities to defraud, either by using the money for personal investment purposes with the ultimate intention of sending some of it overseas when the investments paid off, or else by simply accepting the money with the intention of keeping it all.

The last two decades of the nineteenth century provided Italian bankers with almost unlimited opportunities for exploiting customers. Conditions for depositors improved somewhat after the turn of the century. By the Italian Emigration Law of 1901, the Bank of Naples became designated as the financial institution entrusted by the Italian government with transmission of savings from all parts of the world, including the United States. The bank, therefore, forced many immigrant bankers to improve services for their clients, to modify rates of exchange, and to lower charges for transmission of money.

In addition, after 1900 various states—such as Massachusetts, New York, New Jersey, Pennsylvania, and Ohio—that had large immigrant populations enacted legislation intended to control immigrant banking operations. Nevertheless, the regulations were still far less stringent than those governing state and national banks. In Illinois, rural private bankers effectively opposed rules that might have limited their own free and easy activities.

Early in the immigration, Southern Italians recognized the benefits that accrued in their new homeland from involvement in politics. Political machines in New York, Chicago, New Orleans and other cities granted patronage jobs to Italians (as to members of other immigrant groups as well) in exchange for support on election days. Italians began to move into public employment by at least the early 1890s. Such employment generally offered to unskilled laborers relatively steady income and job security, while to ethnic groups it gave convincing proof of the benefits to be gained from participation in local politics.

After the turn of the century, Italians moved into public employment in ever-increasing numbers even though in the last years of the nineteenth century such work came increasingly under the control of Civil Service Commissions. This was important because it suggested the element of education at a time when tenement dwellers generally did not have much schooling. To Italians and other immigrants civil service meant the loss of a job to a middle-class resident of a neighborhood in the periphery of the city.

Although Italians benefited from opportunities both in public and private employment that made it possible for some to realize great financial success, most Italian immigrants remained laborers throughout their lives. For these men success was achieved if they were able to rise to semiskilled or skilled status. They and their compatriots who remained unskilled laborers contributed substantially but undramatically to the economic growth of the country through work in construction, mining, factory, or maintenance work. The Italian immigrant laborer, S. Merlino wrote in 1893, "tills the soil, builds railroads, bores mountains, drains swamps, opens here and there to the industry of American workmen new fields which would not perhaps be opened but for his cheap labor."[14]

For the typical immigrant the work day was long and the pay was low. A survey conducted by the United States Commissioner of Labor of living and working conditions in Italian neighborhoods of Baltimore, Chicago, New York, and Philadelphia in 1893–94 found that common laborers put in a sixty-hour work week for an average weekly wage of from six to nine dollars. In order to pay for food, housing, clothes, and other necessities (which often were exorbitantly expensive) many found it necessary to put as many members of the family to work as possible. By the age of fourteen, and often earlier, children were removed from school and sent into the job market to supplement the family income. In a break from European habits women went out to work or brought home piecework to do.

In New York, Chicago, and other manufacturing centers, Italian women were heavily represented in the garment industry and in the manufacture of artificial flowers, lace, candy, paper, and tobacco products. As early as 1902 Mabel Hurd Willett, who studied the employment of women in the clothing trades in New York City, found that Italians had gained "a complete monopoly of part of the work, the felling and finishing of ready-made clothing."[15] By 1910 Italian women comprised the largest proportion (36.2 percent) of the female work force in the garment industry in New York City. They dominated the artificial-flower industry, totaling 72 percent of the entire work force in that line of activity. Italian women (along with women of other immigrant groups) went into

Table 7. Processes of Work Performed by Italian Women
Workers in Manufacturing Industries in New York City

Process of Work	Women
Operating sewing machines	222
Feeding and tending machines	64
Fine hand sewing	61
Medium-grade hand sewing	185
Coarse hand sewing	36
Hand and machine processes combined	27
Pasting	90
Branching (flowers and feathers)	45
Cutting	19
Hand stamping	7
Measuring and weighing	9
Sorting	15
Examining	12
Folding	7
Packing	48
Wrapping and tying	8
Ribboning	6
Pressing and cleaning	21
Processes peculiar to certain industries	76
Work incidental to manufacturing, such as supervision and stockkeeping	38
Work not stated further than as "general," or learning	31
Total	1,027[a]

[a] Of the 1,095 women investigated, 68 were not employed in manufacturing industries.

Louise C. Odencrantz, *Women in Industry: A Study of Conditions in New York City* (New York, 1919), p. 51.

this kind of work because the nature of such industries often permitted them to work at home. Production processes were decentralized and the factory work, if the job could not be done at home, required little or no machinery. Such conditions suited women with small children and also made it possible to put girls under sixteen years of age to work.

Whether at home or in a factory, Italian women worked long hours under sweatshop conditions for low pay. In 1895 reformer Jacob Riis described the experience of a New York schoolteacher who decided to visit the home of one of her students because the "little Italian girl, hardly yet out of her teens, stayed away from her class in the Mott Street Industrial School so long" that the teacher was worried. In the girl's apartment the teacher "found the child in a high fever, in bed, sewing on coats with swollen eyes, though barely able to sit up." Sickness, Riis concluded, "unless it be mortal, is no excuse from the drudgery of the tenement."[16] Reformer Florence Wilkinson's outrage at the exploitation of young Italian children prompted her to write a poem entitled "The Flower Factory."

Lisabetta, Marianina, Fiametta, Teresina,
They were winding stems of roses,—one by one, one by one.
Little children who have never learned to play.

High above the clattering street, ambulance and fire-gong beat,
They sit, pasting cotton petals,
One by one, one by one.
Teresina softly crying that her fingers ache today,
Tiny Fiametta nodding when the twilight slips in gray.

Lisabetta, Marianina, Fiametta, Teresina,
They sit curling crimson petals, one by one,
One by one.
They have never seen a rosebud nor a dewdrop in the sun.

They will dream of cotton petals, endless, crimson, suffocating,
Never of a wild rose thicket nor the singing of a cricket,
They will dream of the Vendetta,
Of a black hand through a grating;
And the ambulance will bellow through the wanness of their dreams,
As their tired lids will flutter
With the street's hysteric screams.

Lisabetta, Marianina, Fiametta, Teresina,
They are winding stems of roses,

One by one,
One—by—
One.
Little children who have never learned to play.
Let them have a long long playtime,
Lord of Toil, when toil is done!
Fill their baby hands with roses,
Joyous roses of the sun!

Reprinted in *Poems of Child Labor* (New York, 1924), p. 44.

In 1919 Louise Odencrantz observed that in the prewar era of large-scale immigration "the assertion was frequently heard that the Italian girl underbids her fellow-workers in every occupation she enters, that the most poorly paid home work is largely in her hands, and that Italian standards of living are a menace to American industry."[17] Yet Italian women did not always accept these conditions without complaint. By the eve of World War I they had begun to join labor unions. Although they were less active than Eastern-European Jews, they seemed to be more amenable to organization than Slavic women, or even than native Americans.

Teaching school was the most popular line of employment for middle-class Italian women, particularly those of the second, or American-born, generation. The numbers involved were, however, quite small. Thus of 28 Italians teaching in Chicago in 1914, 24 were female. Women comprised 334 of the 407 Italians teaching in the New York City school system in 1915. Relatively few Italian women worked in any of the professions; most were concentrated in manufacturing. In New York, for example, only some 150 women, or 1.2 percent of all Italian women employed in the city in 1900, were in professional services compared with 9,391, or 77.1 percent, of the Italian working women who in the same year were employed in manufacturing.

Italian men moved into organized labor somewhat earlier than did the women. During the first years of the immigration and before Italians learned American labor practices, they often acted as strikebreakers. As early as 1874 Southern-Italian immigrants were transported into the Pennsylvania coalfields to break a strike. In following years and continuing into the twentieth century new arrivals from the Italian South continued to serve as strikebreakers. For example, in 1882 they helped to break up a strike by freight handlers on the New York docks and railroads and in 1912 they served as strikebreakers for the trunk and valise makers in Chicago. Through such activities, Italians gained an unsavory but not fully deserved reputation as scabs. During the same years, Italians joined existing unions or organized new ones in the stone, garment, and building industries in the eastern areas of the United States. In following years they continued their union interests and activities there and in other parts of the nation.

When they had resided for a time in America, Italians from the South as well as those from the North joined fellow workers (foreign-born and American) in supportting the rights of labor. In 1903, in an early, not fully successful effort at union activity on the part of Italians in America, excavation workers on New York's subways went on strike. Along with Irish, Polish and other workers, Southern Italians, under the leadership of Tito Pacelli, an articulate and intelligent young labor organizer, concluded that their work situation was unbearable. They organized the Rockmen's and Excavators' Union and struck for higher wages, shorter hours, and better job conditions. After more than five weeks of sacrifice the laborers settled for a pay raise of about twenty-five cents a day instead of the seventy-five cents to one dollar a day they had demanded. What was more important, according to Edwin Fenton, was that "they had also gained a union." During the course of the strike, the American Federation of Labor "chartered them as Excavators' Union No. 10,630 and Rockmen's Union No. 10,631, both of which won seats on the Central Federated Union. This formal recognition from the A.F. of L. enabled the Italians to win some successes in the following years."[18] The

1903 strike was just one of the organizational efforts among Italian workers.

Discussing the labor situation in the New York area, historian George Pozzetta has observed that "virtually all trades having large Italian representation experienced labor turmoil during the years after 1900."[19] This included the longshoremen, garment workers, laborers, shoemakers, masons, and bricklayers, to name but a few of the groups.

In addition to supplying rank-and-file support, Italians served as leaders of union locals and even of national organizations. One such organization was the International Hod Carriers' and Building Laborers' Union of America (now the Laborers' International Union of America), formed in 1903 as a member union of the American Federation of Labor. Domenico D'Alessandro of Boston became its general president in 1908 and directed the organization during its early difficult years until his death in 1926, when Chicagoan Joseph V. Moreschi (like D'Alessandro, an Italian immigrant) was elected president.

In the garment trades, Anzuino D. Marimpietri of Chicago, one of the founders of the Amalgamated Clothing Workers of America, served as a vice-president of that union. Under the militant leadership of Luigi Antonini, Salvatore Ninfo, who became a vice-president of the International, and A. Baffa, Italians also entered the International Ladies Garment Workers' Union, and formed powerful ethnic locals in New York City.

Italians produced some of America's foremost radical leaders, among them Arturo Giovannitti and Giuseppe Ettor of the Industrial Workers of the World (the I.W.W.) who led Southern Italian workers in the famous 1912 textile strike in Lawrence, Massachusetts. A cut in wages at the city's textile mills precipitated the Lawrence strike in January 1912. Consisting largely of unskilled immigrants (Italians, Poles, Germans, French, Belgians, French Canadians, Jews, Lithuanians, English, Portuguese, and Syrians), the work force quickly came under the control of the Industrial Workers of the World. Led by Giovannitti, a prominent radical union organizer and editor of the syndicalist-controlled newspaper, *Il Proletario*, and Ettor, a member of the I.W.W. executive board, Italians formed the backbone of the strike. During a fight between police and strikers on January 29, Anna Lo Pezzi, a young Italian woman striker, was shot and killed.

Giovannitti and Ettor were arrested and in September stood trial on the charge of being accessories to murder. After nearly two months of testimony, the anarchist leaders were found innocent but in the process the strike was broken.

Italians moved a long distance from the early years of the immigration when, as Edwin Fenton has shown, "provincialism, fatalism, and self-reliance made it difficult for unions to control them." As Southern Italians moved into organized labor, economic concerns and grievances influenced them rather than philosophical tenets of radicalism and socialism. The key factor in successful immigration organization was "bargaining power"—that is, some assurance that a union might achieve its stated objectives, an assurance that socialists and anarchists often could not offer. Where such prospects existed, Italian immigrants organized rapidly and effectively. They became, in Fenton's words, "faithful members of conservative AFL locals."[20]

One form of economic enterprise that attracted some immigrants and also some members of the second generation and that brought money, if unfavorable publicity, to the Italian community was crime. This included gambling, prostitution, labor racketeering, and the activities of Black Hand extortion gangs.

Writing in 1909, Arthur Woods, Deputy Police Commissioner of New York City, reported that "in almost every case" Black Hand operations were committed by men who had been involved in criminal activities in Italy and who had emigrated to New York in order to continue "fattening off the main body of their fellow-countrymen." During this period, such gangsters had not joined or helped form a tightly organized, centrally directed structure. "The Black Hand is not a cohesive, comprehensive society, working with mysterious signs and passwords," Woods maintained. "Given a number of Italians with money, and two or three ex-convicts, you have all the elements necessary for a first-rate Black Hand campaign."[21]

Black Hand, or *Mano Nera*, activities virtually disappeared in the 1920s, for several reasons. First, the supply of simple, pliable victims dwindled after termination of immigration during World War I and by subsequent restrictive legislation. Second, enforcement of laws prohibiting the use of the mails to defraud forced personal delivery of threatening Black Hand notes. Neighborhood hoodlums, craving anonymity, found this activity to be too risky. While these factors limited opportunities for criminals within the ethnic quarter, at the same time, a vast new field of endeavor had sprung up in the wider American community.

On January 16, 1920, the Eighteenth Amendment and the Prohibition Enforcement Act [Volstead Act] went into effect, forbidding "the manufacture, sale or transportation of intoxicating liquors" for beverage purposes. American tastes and habits did not, however, adjust to the new regulations, and enterprising young men found themselves in a position to reap immense profits. Many well-qualified Black Handers left the less profitable extortion rackets of the Italian quarter in order to move into the more lucrative work of producing and distributing illicit alcohol. But the Black Hand was only one of several sources of personnel for prohibition-era syndicates. During the same decades in which the *Mano Nera* thrived, ambitious young Italian-Americans were in the process of making their way in various other criminal activities.

During the pre-World War I immigrant era the groundwork was laid for the creation of the powerful criminal syndicates that emerged and expanded during the Prohibition era which followed the end of the war. The number of Italians involved in gambling, Black Hand, and other illegal activities before the Prohibition period, or since then for that matter, was small. Nevertheless, the influence they exerted and the power they wielded was far out of proportion to their numbers. This was in part the result of the vast amounts of money they were able to amass. Of even greater importance were the connections they formed with machine politicians and the role they played as power brokers in immigrant-colony and city politics. Thus Jim Colosimo and his nephew John Torrio not only operated a string of prostitution and gambling houses but also helped organize the vote in Chicago's corrupt First Ward for Democratic party machine bosses Michael "Hinky Dink" Kenna and "Bathhouse John" Coughlin. In New York Paul Kelly (Paolo Vaccarelli), who headed the powerful Five Points Gang, played a similar key role in Tammany Hall boss Timothy "Big Tim" Sullivan's organization. Colosimo, Kelly, and others like them recognized that in urban America political activity generally opened the door to economic opportunity.

CHAPTER 6

Politics and the Ladder of Success

Machine politics formed a central aspect of immigrant-colony life. The boss system, a familiar part of the urban scene by the 1880s and 1890s, grew out of conditions in core-area neighborhoods. In 1894 the United States Commissioner of Labor published the results of a survey of slum areas in four major American cities— Baltimore, Chicago, New York, and Philadelphia. In each city investigators found serious overcrowding in tenements, high rents for inferior housing, barely adequate sanitary conditions, and extremely poor social relations. In these neighborhoods, the great numbers of people compounded all existing problems, but in politics, the mass of humanity was a benefit rather than a disadvantage.

When organized and directed, tenement residents proved to be a powerful voice in city affairs. The momentum and organizing power came from ambitious, upwardly mobile members of the second generation who reached maturity only to find economic advancement in the professions and the business world made difficult (but not impossible) by inadequate education, lack of money, and ineffectual family connections. Along with crime and sports, politics offered fame and fortune to slum youngsters despite financial and educational shortcomings.

Immigrant neighborhood political leaders knew the right people to talk to and the right buttons to push to get things done. Those who did not or could not deliver on their promises found their political careers cut short. Political bosses were expected to "fix things up" for their constituents, "the little people," when the need arose.

In the 1930s sociologist William Foote Whyte studied Boston's North End Italian district, which he called "Cornerville," and found in that community that "society is made up of big people and little people—with intermediaries serving to bridge the gaps between them. The masses of Cornerville people are little people. They cannot approach the big people directly, but must have an intermediary to intercede for them."[1]

In exchange for a variety of services and favors, Italians and other core-area residents provided the support on election day that kept ward and city political machines in power. In order to win and to hold immigrant support, bosses made available to a succession of ethnic groups patronage positions with city, county, or state agencies and also jobs with private companies. In fact, Whyte maintained, "the old ward boss owed much of his power to his ability to place men in private industry as well as in government jobs."[2] Work included street cleaning, garbage collecting, custodial jobs in public buildings, road maintenance, and assignments in public transportation networks and sewage systems, besides construction work on tenements, bathhouses, and parks. This employment generally offered unskilled workers relatively steady incomes and job security, while to immigrant groups they gave tangible proof of the benefits to be gained from local politics.

In addition to jobs, the successful political boss obtained exemptions from city ordinances for core-area businessmen; arranged bail and obtained pardons; sponsored dances, parades, picnics, social and athletic affairs, bazaars, and community church functions; distributed turkeys at Thanksgiving and Christmas; gave fuel and food to needy residents; sent flowers to the sick; and attended funerals.

Recipients of patronage positions or favors were obligated to vote for the machine. Although they seldom formed a majority of a ward's eligible voters, they provided a loyal and disciplined nucleus. The high degree of residential mobility displayed by Italians and other immigrants kept many of them from taking an active interest in ward politics. Bosses encouraged this general apathy in order to increase the value of the votes of their loyal followers; hence the ballots of the patronaged few could determine the outcome of an election and, in fact, often did. Social reformer and University of Chicago professor Grace Abbott described how the system of reciprocal personal obligations functioned in Chicago and, by extension, in other cities as well:

One Italian showed me a letter that he said had secured him several jobs. It was from an alderman in the Nineteenth Ward of Chicago whose reign has been long and notorious. It read: "This is a neighbor and a friend of mine. Please give him work." And long after the man has passed from the group of laborers who are dependent upon casual and irregular work and has become the prosperous owner of a grocery store, he will remember his "neighbor and friend" and be glad to do for him any small favor that he can. The only favors asked of him will be at election time, and in his gratitude the Italian will in all probability vote against his own and the city's interest.[3]

Members of the underworld were among the most loyal supporters of the machine. Over the decades an intimate and mutually beneficial relationship developed between urban political machines and underworld organizations. In exchange for a free hand in operating houses of prostitution, saloons, and gambling halls, criminal elements not only helped get out the vote on election day, but also kept many opposition voters from reaching polling stations. In addition, through hoodlum muscle and cash, bosses used intimidation, bribery, violence, and trickery to prevent the rise of effective opposition.

The intimate and mutually beneficial working relationship between urban political machines and criminals formed a cornerstone of New Yorker Timothy D. Sullivan's successful career. In the early 1890s "Big Tim" Sullivan became Bowery Assembly district leader, a position he held into the second decade of the twentieth century.*

The Bowery offered a variety of illegal services to residents and visitors alike. Sullivan permitted gambling dens and houses of prostitution to operate free of police interference. During political campaigns, criminal leaders played important roles in "Big Tim's" political campaigns by guaranteeing the votes of underlings. Gang members, in turn, employed a variety of techniques to cast as many votes as they could without being caught.

By the turn of the century, Italians predominated in the Bowery, and Sullivan cultivated their support by providing jobs, handouts of fuel during harsh winters, and a variety of personal favors. He dramatized his efforts to gain favor among Italians by submitting and helping to secure the passage of a bill making Columbus Day a state holiday. Furthermore, he accepted the takeover by Italian criminals of illicit activities in his district, in exchange for their getting out the vote on election day.

A similar process took place in other core-area election and assembly districts in New York. That process occurred also in the precincts and wards of other cities where Italians, East-European Jews, and other "new" immigrant groups had moved into neighborhoods previously inhabited by Irish, Germans, and other natives of Northern and Western Europe. Knowledgeable political bosses dating from the earlier immigrant waves hung onto their position and power by the shrewd distribution of patronage and political favors, and by accepting the newer groups into their political domains.

In Italian wards, political bosses generally came from Irish backgrounds and found that they needed a contact man or intermediary between themselves and the ethnic masses. The machine

* New York City was divided into assembly districts, each containing from 40,000 to 80,000 inhabitants; assemblies were in turn subdivided into election districts. The assembly district leaders constituted the governing body of the city's Democratic party organization, Tammany Hall.

found it expedient to employ as go-betweens men who spoke the language of the community and who knew customs, prejudices, and the best means of molding opinion and winning votes. One example was Vincent d'Agrosa, who became president of the Columbus Political Club of the Fifth and Eleventh wards in Brooklyn, New York. D'Agrosa was born in Italy, studied for a time in France, and emigrated to the United States by himself at the age of sixteen. He found a job with a furrier in Brooklyn, studied English and other subjects in night school, and in 1888 at the age of twenty-one became an American citizen. D'Agrosa's success in politics grew out of his facility as a linguist. His knowledge of and ability to speak a variety of Italian dialects made it possible for him to communicate with natives of various provinces and towns of Italy and to weld them together into a political organization under his direction and control.

Often intermediaries such as d'Agrosa caught the boss's attention by organizing a segment of the colony, perhaps a benefit society or a group of fellow workers or even a group of relatives and friends, and leading them to the polls to vote. Such leaders became small cogs in the ward machine, but they held power within the ethnic district because their recommendations meant patronage jobs for friends and lack of employment for enemies. For ambitious men, control of votes in the immigrant quarter could be turned to personal advantage, either to obtain more important positions within the machine or to establish competing organizations. Winning elective office or exerting political influence became a means of gaining esteem within the ward and also American recognition of Italian influence.

Despite diligent efforts Italians enjoyed limited political success in the decades prior to World War I. Robert F. Foerster noted this fact in 1919, when he observed that their achievement was at the ward and, occasionally, city level, but rarely were they elected or appointed to a state office. "In national affairs," he correctly judged, "the Italians have so far been all but negligible."[4]

A major problem for most Italian candidates in elections above the ward level in the immigration era and even later was the inability of the Italian group alone to insure electoral success. Italian voters generally heeded the advice of their press and other community leaders and cast their votes for fellow Italians, regardless of party affiliation. In order to gain elective office, however, candidates found it necessary to attract voters of other ethnic groups. Quite simply, there were not enough registered Italian voters in any large American city during the immigration era to guarantee by themselves the election of Italian candidates for such offices as mayor, governor, or state or federal legislator.

Italians, Greeks, Poles, and other "new" immigrant groups had a lower percentage of naturalization than did the earlier groups from Northern and Western Europe. In the period from 1899 to 1910, according to the United States Immigration Commission, only 15.7 percent of the Southern-Italian immigrants in the country were naturalized, compared with 25.3 percent for Northern Italians, 22.7 percent for East-European Jews, 21.1 percent for Poles, and 12.1 percent for Slovaks. The lower naturalization figures among Southern and Eastern Europeans resulted from the short span of time since their arrival in the United States and their unfamiliarity with the economic and social advantages accruing from citizenship and involvement in politics.

Heavy concentrations of Italian immigrants and their children did not, however, automatically insure political success. Irish bosses were adept at retaining control of core-area wards that had long before shifted from Northern-European to Southern-European voting majorities.

Typical of the problems Italians had in winning elective office in the early years of immigration even in wards containing sizable Italian populations were the difficulties encountered by opponents of Chicago's Nineteenth Ward alderman John Powers. In nearly forty years as a ward boss in Chicago (1889 to 1927), Powers used any means necessary to retain political influence. Reformer Jane Addams, who challenged Powers's control of the ward from her position as head of Hull House Settlement House, concluded that Powers remained boss because of the services he rendered. Most important, Addams believed, he used his prominence in city politics and his influence with businessmen to get jobs for constituents. Besides jobs, he provided the usual benefits and services, from furnishing bond for ward residents charged with crimes to supporting church functions and attending funerals. In return for his many kindnesses, Powers asked for only one thing: votes at election time.

Despite the outward appearance of absolute control over his domain Powers could never rest comfortably on his laurels. In fact he was in constant danger of losing control and regularly found it necessary to resort to the use of force and fraud at elections and the promise, which he regularly broke, of political office to buy opponents.

Contrary to Addams's analysis, Powers did not preside effectively over his constituents' well-being, nor did he attempt to do so. Dirt and refuse filled the streets of the Nineteenth Ward. The area desperately needed parks and bathhouses. Hull House investigators found public schools badly overcrowded and poorly equipped, with three thousand more children than seats available for them. Hull House reformers determined to improve the situation by opposing Powers and his henchmen, but found themselves easily outmaneuvered. Powers won the election of 1898, when Hull House and the Italian community organized to fight him. He lost but one of thirty-three precincts, the seventeenth, which contained the highest concentration of Italian voters in the ward. Oscar Durante, editor and publisher of *L'Italia*, claimed that this vote signaled a declaration of war against Powers on the part of the ward's Italians. Although Jane Addams and the Hull House reformers gave up the struggle after the 1898 debacle the city's Italian-language press and other community leaders continued to fight Powers until 1921. All their efforts failed.

Only one Italian-American leader mounted an effective challenge to the ward boss, and that duel lasted from 1915 until the final defeat of the anti-Powers forces in the aldermanic election of

1921. The Italian leader, Anthony D'Andrea, was a convicted counterfeiter, unfrocked priest, and alleged criminal boss. D'Andrea's political strength lay in the labor organizations he headed or served as business agent. His weakness, which he never was able to overcome, was his unsavory background. Not even a reputation as the "Mafia leader of Chicago" was enough to guarantee electoral success.[5] The women of the ward—who were enfranchised in 1913 in Illinois—repudiated him in favor of Powers, who posed successfully as a humble, church-going family man. Powers won the male vote with a plurality of 124 and the female vote by 257, out of a total of 7,587 votes. D'Andrea died from a shotgun blast less than three months after the election, a grim warning to other politically ambitious Italians.

In contrast to the anti-Powers forces who, although they totaled 70 percent of the ward's registered voters by 1921, were ineffectual and consistently outmaneuvered their compatriots in the First Ward, led by James Colosimo, forged the city's most powerful Italian political organization. The political bosses of the ward, "Hinky Dink" Kenna and "Bathhouse John" Coughlin, ruled a domain inhabited by more than twenty-five nationalities. At no time before or after the turn of the century did the Italian element approach a majority of residents or of registered voters in the ward. In the years after 1900 "Big Jim" Colosimo welded the Italian element into a highly effective voting bloc that exerted an influence far beyond its mere numbers. A shrewd realist, "Big Jim" avoided a destructive confrontation with the ward's Irish political bosses like that between Powers and D'Andrea. Until his death in 1920 Colosimo remained in the background as Irish politicians retained control of elective offices. In exchange, "Big Jim" and his successors in the 1920s, John Torrio and Al Capone, enjoyed complete freedom from police and other officials for criminal operations in the ward.

Prior to the 1920s a scattering of Italian Americans won elective office in Chicago and other cities, but significant successes only occurred on a regular basis during and after the 1930s. In the early years of political activity Italians were to be found in both the Republican and Democratic parties. It was not until the 1930s, because of the impact of the Great Depression and the social legislation of the New Deal, that Italians and other "new" immigrant groups, moved en masse into the ranks of the Democratic party. Prior to that time, as one writer has observed, "Italians were distributed from the extreme left to the extreme right."[6]

On the political left Italians figured prominently in the activities of most of the radical organizations. Arturo Giovannitti, who played a major role in the I.W.W.-led Lawrence strike of 1912, became an ardent socialist and devoted the rest of his life to a struggle against the oppressions of the established order. Other prominent socialist leaders included Augusto Bellanca, Salvatore Ninfo, Giuseppe Bertelli, and Luigi Antonini. Right-wing elements did not coalesce into a unified element until the 1920s with the emergence in Italy of Benito Mussolini and Fascism. A Fascist League of America was organized in 1925 but the group was disbanded before the end of the decade.

Organizations of both the extreme right and left created a great deal of sound and motion but offered little of substance to the general public. The great majority of the immigrants and their children were generally not interested in radical or reactionary ideas or political movements. Instead they turned either to the Republican or the Democratic party to help them in their efforts to deal with the everyday problems of life in urban America, such as obtaining jobs, exemptions from the law, neighborhood facilities (such as bathhouses), and numerous other services and facilities. As a result, "in any particular election the Italian vote may sway this way or that, under the influence of temporary factors that swing elections everywhere."[7]

The experience of two Lower East Side New York Italian bosses, James March and Paul Kelly, demonstrates how turn-of-the-century city political machines operated and illustrates the career opportunities available to shrewd, ambitious, and ruthless immigrant youngsters. March, born Antonio Maggio in a village in

Lucania in Southern Italy, arrived in the United States in 1873, a penniless youngster of thirteen. Before the end of his flamboyant career the self-styled "Mayor of Lafayette Street," according to one authority, "achieved fame and fortune . . . and became a power in the degraded political life of the East Side." He was a familiar figure in the saloons and meeting halls of Lafayette, Mulberry, and other streets in the Lower East Side where "the ward heelers and the local underworld admired him tremendously."[8]

March began his career in America as an unskilled railroad laborer. By 1880 he had settled in New York City and started a prosperous association with the Erie Railroad, which he served as a labor agent. A story told of his work as a padrone illustrated as well the factors responsible for his success in politics. It was said that on one occasion the Erie Railroad placed a rush order with March to recruit one thousand Italian workers for construction work some distance from the city. With the aid of his many contacts, a glib tongue, and extravagant promises he filled the order within hours. For his services not only did March receive a commission from the company but he collected a fee of eight dollars from each of the thousand workers.

Over the years March became a prosperous businessman, trustee of an Italian bank, owner of extensive amounts of property, and an influential politician. From 1894 until his death in 1910 March exerted political influence as Republican party leader in the Third Assembly, or Bowery, district on New York's Lower East Side.

March was credited with controlling the Italian vote in his district and was rewarded accordingly by the Republican party hierarchy. In 1897 he was appointed warden of the Port of New York, a position ripe with potential for patronage and graft, by the governor of New York State (and soon to be the Vice-President and then President of the United States), Theodore Roosevelt, who was one of March's many friends. March became a Presidential elector in 1904 and by 1908 was county leader of the Republican party.

Despite the prominence and prestige he enjoyed and the many benefits he received, March and the Republican party were never very important in the Bowery. As George Pozzetta has noted, "much of March's success was more apparent than real" because all through his career "the district over which he presided was solidly Democratic and long considered to be Tammany territory."[9]

The real Italian political boss of the Bowery was March's counterpart in the Democratic party, Paul Kelly. Christened Paolo Antonio Vaccarelli in his native Naples, he took the name Paul Kelly during an early boxing career shortly after emigrating with his parents to New York. Unlike the husky and powerful-looking March, who looked the part of a political leader, Kelly was small, dapper, well bred, soft-spoken, and fluent in four languages. He resembled anything but the popular image of a machine boss and criminal gang leader, but during his long and varied career he was both.

By the turn of the century Kelly was an important cog in "Big Tim" Sullivan's machine which controlled politics on New York's Lower East Side. The basis of Kelly's power and influence was his position as leader of the Five Points Gang, a veritable army of fifteen hundred youths composed largely of Italians but also including Jews, Irish, and members of other ethnic groups. On election day Kelly's forces would fan out through the Lower East Side and herd voters to the polls to vote for Tammany-endorsed candidates. Among Kelly's followers were Charles "Lucky" Luciano, Al Capone, and John Torrio, himself leader of a neighborhood gang, the James Street Boys, who during the 1920s would become a Chicago syndicate leader and architect of the organization Capone would later head.

The effects of years of destructive gang warfare with another huge Lower East Side gang led by a vicious apelike psychopath named Monk Eastman which sapped the strength of the Kelly Forces, combined with the pressure that reform groups applied after 1900 to curb the power of urban political machines, helped persuade Kelly it was time to widen his horizons. While continuing to maintain his connections, and thus remaining a political power in the Lower East Side, Kelly in the years after 1910 began to involve himself in unionization. He first organized the ragpickers, then became leader of a group of harbor unions, and later a vice-president of the International Longshoremen's Association.

Like most political bosses of the era Kelly and March wielded power and exerted what influence they could behind the scenes. Neither man was ever a candidate for elective office and both would probably have gone down to defeat if they ever had embarked on a campaign in their own behalf.

The transient nature of much of the Italian population in the years before 1914 and the employment of many in railroad and other construction work that kept them out of New York, Chicago, and other cities during much of the year delayed or prevented large numbers of the newcomers from becoming citizens, registering, and voting. In any case, many of them intended to return to Italy. The Italian government, far from encouraging emigrants to adjust to a new homeland, opposed their adopting "the citizenship of the country where they reside."[10] The Italian-language press in the United States strongly disagreed with this attitude of the Kingdom and advised immigrants that while they should take pride in their Italian heritage, they ought to adjust in every possible way to their new homeland.

When Italian immigrants did register and vote they generally did so in national elections. In 1905 the Chicago Italian-language newspaper *L'Italia* commented that "the Italian laborers, . . . while they become agitated and excited when faced with a Presidential election, remain later indifferent when the elections concern the municipality."[11] Studies by University of Chicago political scientists Harold Gosnell and Charles Merriam on the problem of non-participation in Chicago local elections found that indifference and inertia were the principal factors responsible for Italians (immigrant and American-born alike) not voting. Gosnell and Merriam found that this was not unique to the Italian group. Indifference was the major factor in nonvoting of all groups examined, which included English and Canadian, Irish, German, Scandinavian, Russian, Polish and that designated as "Other Slavic," as well as Italian. However, the Italian percentage was higher (32 percent) than that of any other group except Other Slavic (35.8 percent).[12]

The average Italian voter, an unskilled laborer, concerned himself primarily with economic issues. It appeared to him that these issues were decided at the national level. While national campaigns held the glamour and excitement often lacking in municpal and state elections, local politics yielded the more immediate—and perhaps more important—results. Only the bosses, the recipients of political favors and patronage, and interest groups (like community businessmen) fully realized this fact and made effective use of the vote to their own advantage.

Contributing to political indifference was the circumstance that in most cities Italians lacked able and attractive candidates—men who had an appeal for voters outside the Italian community. Two Italian Americans who enjoyed great political success were Anthony Caminetti and Fiorello La Guardia, but they were exceptions.

Anthony Caminetti had a long and distinguished career in California and national politics. Like so many other early immigrants to California, Caminetti's parents arrived in the state during the Gold Rush. Anthony was born in 1854 in Amador County and although his father was a successful farmer the youngster worked his way through college and immediately embarked on a career in politics. In 1877 he was elected district attorney of Amador County, a position he held until 1882, when he won a seat in the state legislature. A lifelong Democrat, Caminetti served in the state senate from 1887 until 1890, when he became a member of the United States House of Representatives. After serving two terms in Washington, Caminetti returned to California in 1895 to run a successful campaign for state senator. From 1907 to 1913 he served yet another term in the state senate. In 1913 he embarked upon the final phase of his public career.

With the election of Woodrow Wilson as President, Caminetti returned to Washington as Commissioner of Immigration. The two terms he served in Wilson's cabinet should have been a happy time for Caminetti but it was not. A history of the Department of Labor evaluated Caminetti's tenure in office in this way: "Of all the commissioners-general up to that time Caminetti was the most unfortunate. A student of administrative organization observed that his inexpert administration of his office was nerveless to the point almost of paralysis."[13] Even more damaging than his administrative shortcomings was Caminetti's handling of dissenters and radicals during World War I and after. During a period of ardent antiradicalism Caminetti, according to William Preston, "seemed anxious to prove his own loyalty by an all-out attack on immigrants suspected of subversion."[14] In light of his role in fanning the flames of fear and hatred during the postwar Red Scare, Andrew Rolle has concluded that Caminetti's influence on immigrants and immigration was negative. "Here was an Italian," Rolle notes, "who, though he never renounced his immigrant background, used it in a manner totally at variance with the spirit of non-restrictive immigration that had allowed his very parents to come to America."[15] It is important to recognize, however, that this did not represent a shift in Caminetti's attitude. While still a member of the California legislature he played a prominent role in the passage of the Chinese Exclusion Bill. To state it simply, Caminetti was not a typical Italian American of his generation. He was college educated at a time when most youngsters did not even finish grammar school; was a Protestant, and identified strongly with the economic establishment of California and the nation.

Fiorello La Guardia was another atypical Italian American who, unlike Caminetti, strove throughout his political career to aid and protect all of the needy and downtrodden in urban America. La Guardia's political success was, in fact, based on his uniqueness, on a set of factors that distinguished him from the typical big-city ethnic politician and that for many diverse reasons appealed to a wide range of voters. In the words of his biographer Arthur

Mann, La Guardia was "a marginal man who lived on the edge of
so many cultures, so that he was able to face in several directions
at the same time."[16] Born in New York's Greenwich Village of an
Italian father and a Jewish mother, La Guardia was raised in
Arizona, where his father served as an army bandmaster. In religion an Episcopalian, La Guardia married a Catholic and after her
death, a Lutheran. La Guardia was a passionate, emotional, and
flamboyant man who devoted his life to a fight against corruption,
injustice, exploitation, and intolerance. He combined, as Howard
Zinn has noted, "a profound sense of social responsibility with an
irrepressible individualism. He was a rebel, but not a nihilist, a
man who smashed wildly through party and organizational walls,
but only to follow his principles wherever they led."[17]

As a young man La Guardia worked as a file clerk at the American consulate in Budapest and, after three years there, was promoted to consul agent in Fiume, a one-man branch agency under
the jurisdiction of the Budapest consulate. He soon found, however, that even though he attended language classes to learn to
speak Italian, German, French, and Yiddish, his hopes for advancement were blocked by his lack of formal schooling, so he
resigned his post and returned to America to gain a formal education. During the day La Guardia worked as an interpreter at Ellis
Island and at night took courses at New York University's law
school. In 1909 he received his law degree and was admitted to the
bar. He soon gained a reputation for being more concerned with
accepting cases of clients he considered innocent than with the size
of his fees. In fact, he often offered his services to the poor for
free. His trademarks were honesty, integrity, and a deep concern
for the rights of the weak and the poor. It was not long before he
formed a deep dislike for Tammany Hall and all that organization
stood for in the city of New York. He began to take an active part
in local Republican Club activities with an eye to running for a
seat in the United States House of Representatives. The opportunity presented itself in 1914 and La Guardia became a candidate
for an open seat from the Fourteenth Congressional District, which

included the large Lower East Side Italian community, a long-time Tammany stronghold.

Even in his first political campaign, Arthur Mann has observed, La Guardia displayed characteristics that would distinguish his later career. "He was, on the one hand, sensitive to the suffering of the underprivileged but, on the other, as bruisingly rough and tumble as the best Tammany in-fighters."[18] He was badly beaten but still made a better showing than anyone, except La Guardia himself, thought possible. He was rewarded for his efforts with an appointment as a deputy attorney general of the State of New York, working in New York City, a position he held for a year and a half while he laid the groundwork for another try for the Fourteenth District Congressional seat. In 1916 he won his first elective office, a seat in the United States Congress as a Republican from a district that was traditionally Democratic. Although successful Italian-American politicians in the East and Middle West generally were machine candidates who worked closely with ward, city, and state bosses and therefore opposed reform, La Guardia was throughout his career an outspoken and independent reformer.

In March 1917 La Guardia took his seat in Congress, the first Republican to serve his district since the Civil War. A month later the United States declared war against Germany and in July, just four months after entering Congress, La Guardia took a leave of absence from the House to enlist as a first lieutenant in the Aviation Section of the Signal Corps. He served with distinction in Italy and by August 1918 was a major. On October 28, 1918, one week before election day, he returned to New York to fight for his Congressional seat. He won the election in a landslide, resigned his army commission, and returned to Washington, but only for a brief period. In 1919 Republican leaders prevailed upon the Italian-American war hero to return to New York City and run for the office of president of the Board of Aldermen, the second highest executive position in the city government. La Guardia agreed but only after receiving assurances that he would be the party's choice two years later in the contest for mayor.

La Guardia won the election in 1919 for president of the Board of Aldermen which gave him "the unique distinction of being the first Republican to win a city-wide municipal election in New York without fusion backing."[19] The victory was significant as well for Italian Americans throughout the United States. President of the Board of Aldermen of New York City was the most important elective position that any Italian had gained to that time in a major American city. With this achievement La Guardia became a source of pride for all Italian Americans. He was, as one newspaper put it, "the man of the moment."

As president of the Board of Aldermen La Guardia did an effective job and picked up valuable experience in the conduct of city government that would serve him well in later years. Unfortunately he clashed with party leaders and in the 1921 mayoral primary they denied him the nomination. He had become, with his outspoken criticisms of the Republican governor and state legislature, support of striking shoe workers in New York City, and denunciations of excessive profits for the telephone company, "a political nuisance."[20] His political career, which had seemed so promising just two years before, now appeared to be ended. Yet just one year later he would be back in the limelight. In 1922, his differences with the Republican hierarchy smoothed over, and with the party's blessings, La Guardia sought and won the seat he had earlier held in Congress.

La Guardia served in the House of Representatives from 1923 to 1933, when he returned to New York and, running against a nationwide trend to the Franklin D. Roosevelt–led Democratic party, won the office of mayor. For the next twelve years (1933 to 1945), the heyday of the New Deal, the Republican La Guardia provided New York with honest, efficient, and dynamic leadership. He did not, however, enjoy the distinction of being the first Italian American to serve as mayor of a major American city. In 1931 Angelo Rossi, son of Genoese immigrants, became mayor of San Francisco and served in that office until 1944. Nevertheless, La

Guardia's career reflected the coming of age of Italian Americans in city politics.

An able, dynamic, and reform-minded leader like Fiorello La Guardia could weld together the Italian element and also attract voters from other ethnic groups. In the decades before the 1930s and 1940s such men were seldom to be found in politics. In their absence the political field was, almost by default, left to machine politicians and their underworld allies and associates whose major, if not sole, concern was winning elections and thus gaining the power, influence, and patronage that in American cities went with such success.

Fortunately, Italian immigrants were not dependent solely upon the largesse or the whim of political bosses. A variety of institutions existed that helped serve the needs of immigrants and their children. Some institutions functioned within the Italian colony. Others, like political machines, social settlements, and public schools operated in the larger American environment. The next chapter will examine the role and functions of community institutions, and the family will be discussed in the chapter following.

CHAPTER 7

The Fabric of Immigrant Life: The Community

Native Americans often mistakenly assumed that ethnic districts and institutions reproduced homeland surroundings and perpetuated isolated group life. In actuality, the immigrant community and its institutions represented an important step *away* from Old World patterns. Family-centered in Europe, the newcomers remained so in the United States, but they soon discovered that the family unit was unable to deal effectively with most of the problems encountered in urban America. They had to cooperate with other newcomers and other family groups in order to survive. The community awareness and group consciousness that developed through this cooperation did not arrive with the immigrants but developed in the New World in response to the American environment. "In America," sociologist Robert E. Park reported, "the peasant discards his [Old World] habits and acquires 'ideas.' In America, above all, the immigrant organizes. These organizations are the embodiment of his new needs and his new ideas."[1]

Because the city prevented isolation, the community and its institutions were neither fully European nor fully American in character. Constantine Panunzio, himself an immigrant and a community leader, noted this when he described an Italian colony in which he resided in Boston as being "in no way a typical American community, [but] neither did it resemble Italy."[2] Immigrants attempted to cling to what was familiar from the European village, but in the American urban environment they found it impossible to re-create village life; yet they, and most Americans, believed that they had done so. Edith Abbott and Sophonisba P. Breckinridge, both reformers and college professors, voiced their apprehension in 1912. They feared that through "churches and schools, and in social, fraternal and national organizations," immigrants could maintain "the speech, the ideals, and to some extent the manner of life of the mother country."[3]

Despite American anxieties, community institutions of the various immigrant groups in the United States more closely resembled each other and native American counterparts than they did homeland organizations, which were essentially middle class in origin and character and seldom touched the lives of the groups from which immigrants came. Within Italian districts, three institutions emerged that sought to offer guidance and leadership for community residents: these were the mutual-benefit societies, the Church, and the Italian-language press. Two other institutions, the immigrant bank and the padrone labor system, sought financial profit and—unlike the Church, press, and societies—made no claims about contributing to group welfare. After making fortunes from exploitation of fellow Italians, many padrones and bankers later emerged as immigrant colony leaders (or *prominenti*), but benevolence was neither their original purpose nor their main goal.

Many immigrants turned to mutual-benefit societies to help them deal with the complexities of life in their new homeland. In Southern Italy the family provided aid in time of need. Group life consisted of a few small and unimportant social clubs featuring recreational activities. By the 1890s mutual-aid societies began to appear in the Italian South where they were closely involved in the growth of labor unions. In the United States societies concentrated primarily on insurance and social functions, aiding newly arrived immigrants to deal with sickness, loneliness, and death, but they also served as "the beginnings, however frail, of a cooperative system and of organized labor."[4] Benefit societies existed in this country long before the Italian immigrant era. They were apparently an outgrowth of the English friendly societies, although native-American groups developed a stronger social and fraternal character than their English predecessors possessed.

The immigrant fraternal lodge filled a great social and psychological void for those uprooted from familiar surroundings and life patterns. In the view of Edwin Fenton this function was so important that it made societies "the key institutions of Italian-America," a claim that advocates of the role of the press and of the Catholic Church would dispute.[5] Thus Italian-American journalist Luigi Carnovale, who worked for papers in Chicago and St. Louis, firmly maintained that the foreign-language press was the immigrant's best and truest friend in America. "The colonial press has, in brief, always provided Italian immigrants all that is indispensable—good advice, moral and material assistance, true and ardent fraternal love—for their success" in the new homeland.[6]

Northern Italians in East Coast cities early on formed societies. *The Società di Unione e Benevolenza Italiana*, organized around 1825 in New York City, was apparently the first. The purpose of the society was to provide aid for the poor, the sick, and the needy in the colony and "to keep alive a true feeling of nationality."[7] Some organizations also formed in San Francisco, Philadelphia, Boston, and a few other large cities in the 1850s and 1860s, but it was during the decades of Southern-Italian immigration that mutual-aid societies proliferated. The early organizations prospered and increased in membership and influence and "then, like amoebae, they divided and divided again while hundreds of independent societies sprang up beside them."[8]

Although the pioneer societies of the pre-1870 era contained members from various parts of Italy, those that were formed during the period of large-scale immigration generally were based on place of origin, either town or province of birth. Early groups were small, financially weak, and short-lived. There was a profusion of organizations; new groups sprang into existence only to go quickly out of business. As historian Caroline Ware observed, "the number of these societies was legion, and even their names were often not known outside of their own membership."[9] At the turn of the century Italian colonies on the island of Manhattan supported more than 150 mutual-aid societies. Springfield, Massachusetts, with an Italian population of 2,915 in 1910, had twelve benefit groups.

In time small units consolidated or joined larger ones, and Italian heritage rather than town of birth or place of residence became prerequisites. The largest and most influential organization in the country, the Order Sons of Italy in America, was started in New York City in June 1905 by Dr. Vincent Sellaro. By 1923 the Sons of Italy was nationwide in scope, numbering nearly 300,000 members in 1,190 lodges.

Italians who joined immigrant-era mutual-benefit societies contributed small monthly sums, usually between twenty-five and sixty cents, to guarantee that the group would look after them when they were sick and bury them when they died. Constitutions and bylaws required members to attend funeral services or pay a fine, thus assuring each member a proper burial and a well-attended service. Societies also handled other activities, particularly the payments of sickness and accident expenses. A long-lived Springfield, Massachusetts, Italian mutual-aid society was described in the organization's annual report for 1914 as a society that "unites us and gives us strength, and will make us more acceptable in the eyes of the American people; that will guide us in all vicissitudes and troubles of life; that will give us work when we are idle; that will succor us with money when we are sick; that will help our families and accompany us with dignified ceremony when we die." The group celebrated its twenty-fifth anniversary in 1914 with a membership of four hundred men, a fund of $3,500, and a record of disbursements in payments to the sick and death benefits of approximately $15,000.[10]

New York Italian-colony leader Gino Speranza described the benefits provided by societies in that city in a March 8, 1904, article he wrote for the New York *Times*. According to Speranza services included "doctor's care, the nursing by fellow members and a weekly payment for a few months of from five to seven dollars. Chronic cases [were] sent to their native town, receiving, besides their fare, a lump sum, generally fifty dollars." In order to attract and hold membership, mutual-aid groups found it necessary to expand their services from basic benefit functions to include social ones as well, among them provision for recreational facilities and special annual events like picnics, dances, and religious celebrations. The aims of the Sons of Italy, as reported by the Foreign Language Information Service in 1923, reflected the broadened scope and objectives of societies by the twenties. "In addition to serving as an insurance agency for its members" the Sons of Italy aimed "to promote understanding between Italians and the rest of the community, to cultivate loyalty to the adopted country, to raise the standards of citizenship and to prepare candidates for citizenship."[11] A commemorative publication proclaimed the strong American cast of the organization even more forcefully: "The 'Order Sons of Italy' stands for the best American Ideals contained in our Constitution."[12]

Italian immigrants found a surprisingly wide choice of entertainment available in urban America, especially in New York City. In addition to the neighborhood saloon and the functions and facilities of mutual-aid societies, newcomers could participate in religious festivals and attend plays and vaudeville performances, puppet and marionette shows, and the opera. They could also read Italian-language newspapers and magazines, and by the 1930s, listen to foreign-language radio programs; or they could read from a growing list of novels, poems, and nonfiction describing and attempting to explain the immigrant experience.

Like other European peasants, Southern-Italian immigrants brought folk customs and beliefs with them to the United States. Prominent among the traditions Italians carried to America was the celebration of religious festivals. In 1900 settlement worker Charlotte Kimball described the social activities of Italian immigrants in New York City in *Charities* magazine. She noted that "twenty or more" religious festivals "are still annually observed here by means of elaborate processions of holy brothers, brass bands, sacred images, paper-trimmed floats, veiled girls with candles and affiliated church associations." Kimball found that the festivals were elaborately planned and organized and "when the day arrives the line of march is thronged, the crowd stands bareheaded and devout, but the appreciation of the gay colors, the music, and the presence of their children and friends in the show is keen. Their saints' parade," she concluded, "is to them what a returned hero's parade is to us—a bond, a reminder, and the thrill of the uncommonplace."[13] Immigrants celebrated these functions not only in an effort to re-establish those elements of religion that had strongly appealed to them in the homeland, but also to counteract Irish influences, which seemed to them to make the American Church impersonal, indifferent, and rigid. Some of the religious celebrations, like the festival of San Gennaro on New York's Lower East Side, are still held annually.

During festivals and other special days, immigrants dressed in their colorful native costumes and danced the folk dances of their town or district in Southern Italy. Except on such occasions, newcomers attempted to dress, dance, and behave like other Americans. They quickly learned to ridicule and deride recent arrivals who looked like foreigners.

Although several Italian dishes—foremost among them pizza—became American favorites, at the turn of the century they were looked upon unfavorably. To social workers and the general public, Italians who ate macaroni and drank red wine were offering proof that they had not yet become true Americans. Even so, most immigrants remained loyal to their traditional foods, and the production or importation from Italy of olive oil, spaghetti, artichokes, salami, and other foodstuffs became an important basis of the ethnic colony's economic well-being. In large part the immigrants craved Old World dishes because only in the new homeland could they afford them. The traditional diet of Southern-Italian peasants consisted almost entirely of corn and wheat products, vegetables, and fruits. Only on special occasions could peasants in Italy afford meat or chicken. In America, immigrants enjoyed a diet which—as a 1908 Italian government report observed—was "more abundant, varied, and rich" than was typical in the homeland.[14]

New York City, with the largest Italian community in the United States, was the center of immigrant culture in this country. Theater professor A. Richard Sogliuzzo has noted that New York "once had a thriving theatre which served a large segment of the city's Italian-speaking population."[15] The Italian-American theater arrived in the city during the 1880s and early theatrical activity was centered in amateur theater clubs. Among the first groups, according to Sogliuzzo, were the *Circolo filodrammatico italo-Americano* (1885), *Compagnia Galileo Galilei* (1890), and the *Compagnia filodrammatica napoletana* (1891). The popularity and success enjoyed by these and other clubs encouraged professional actors to migrate to the United States.

The most important figure in the early history of the Italian-American theater was Antonio Maiori, a native of Sicily, who arrived in New York in 1892 at the age of twenty-four. An excellent actor, Maiori dominated the legitimate theater from 1898 to the beginning of World War I. His specialty was Italianized adaptations of Shakespeare's plays and he gained particular success in *Hamlet* and *Othello*.

Although the legitimate theater boasted a number of effective actors and actresses, it did not enjoy the popularity of vaudeville, where an audience favorite was the brilliant comedian Eduardo Migliaccio, who used the stage name Farfariello, or "Little Butterfly". Migliaccio was born in 1880 into a well-to-do family at Cava dei Tireni near Naples. The family emigrated to Pennsylvania in 1898. The young Eduardo soon moved to New York where he found employment in a Lower East Side immigrant bank. He frequently spent his lunch hours at a nearby Italian music hall, the Vittorio Emmanuale, and "one afternoon, quite spontaneously, entertained the audience with a song and a comic sketch. . . . His success was instantaneous, and he became a regular performer at the Vittorio Emmanuale." Although he had no formal theatrical training, Migliaccio was strongly attracted to acting and possessed enormous natural talent. Equally important was a driving ambition to fully develop and channel his talents and a huge capacity for hard work. As Farfariello he specialized in character sketches drawn from life in New York's Little Italy. The sketches, which Farfariello conceived and wrote as well as performed, grew out of and described the immigrant experience in America. He was famous for "his depiction of the *Cafone*, the country bumpkin helplessly adrift in the New World," a role Sogliuzzo believes "was comparable to Chaplin's tramp; the little guy full of good intentions and ambitions, but victimized both by society and his own ineptitude."[16] Another student of the Italian theater found Farfariello to be "a blend of fourteenth-century Italian harlequin and the modern pantomine style of Charlie Chaplin."[17]

Acting troupes frequently went on tour. Maiori's company performed in San Francisco from 1910 to 1912, and Farfariello was there in 1917 and 1918 during a highly successful national tour. San Francisco, as well as other large cities, supported its own Italian-theater groups although not as successfully as New York, which had the advantage of a huge and constantly replenished immigrant population. In other cities professional Italian theater generally appeared for the first time shortly after 1900, reached a peak of popularity in the years just prior to World War I, and went into decline in the postwar years as immigration, owing to restrictive federal legislation, dwindled. In San Francisco, for example, professional Italian theater made its debut on April 9, 1905, when Antonietta Pisanelli "and a troupe of hastily-gathered amateur performers" presented "a varied program of songs and sketches." The widely acclaimed Neapolitan singer remained in San Francisco where she soon became "the Italian colony's first impresario" of variety theater.[18] Her venture blossomed in the following decade, but by 1925, only twenty years after its birth, the Italian theater in the city was dead. This brief lifespan was typical of the Italian theater in American cities. The exception to the general pattern was New York City, which continued to receive most of

the new immigrants to the country, and where Italian theater existed into the 1950s.

The Italian-American theater appealed to immigrant audiences.
As immigration decreased in volume and the immigrant generation
aged and died out, the threater declined. Even during the immigrant era, however, opera, music halls, and marionette shows had
an even greater appeal for Italian Americans than did the legitimate or the popular theater. While the regular theater's price of
admission ranged from ten to fifty cents, admission to the music
hall or vaudeville performance was free. Profits, which were substantial, came from the price of drinks. Customers flocked in for
the presentation of Neapolitan songs and dances. Marionette theater was, in the opinion of Elisabeth Irwin, "the most Italian thing"
the immigrants "brought with them."[19] And, Charlotte Kimball
reported in 1900, the immigrants ardently supported this form of
entertainment. At the Teatro del Marionetta, in New York's
Lower East Side, audiences of up to 175 men, women, and children paid from ten to twenty cents to view a performance. The
principal appeal of these shows, in addition to their similarity to
presentations the audiences had been familiar with in Italy, was
that they were excellent entertainment for the entire family.

Opera also held a powerful appeal for turn-of-the-century immigrants. According to one writer of the time, J. M. Scanland, "Italians look upon opera as a necessity, and also strictly as an amuse-
ment. And they want it strong and good, artistically and musically.
They care little for scenery—they want the acting, and upon this
and the music everything depends."[20] Unlike music-hall performers, opera singers and musicians generated an appeal beyond
the Italian colony. From the 1880s, when the Metropolitan Opera
House opened with Cleofante Campanini as its first orchestra
leader and director, until recent years, Italians dominated opera in
the United States. Two events of major importance were the American debut at the Metropolitan on November 23, 1903, of Nea-
politan-born Enrico Caruso, perhaps the most famous of all opera
singers, and the appointment in 1908 of Giulio Gatti-Casazza,

formerly of Milan's La Scala, as general manager of the Metropolitan Opera Company. Under Gatti-Casazza and even after his retirement in 1934, the Metropolitan brought the most talented performers in Italy to New York. These included Amelita Galli-Curci, Luisa Tetrazzini, Antonio Scotti, Titta Ruffo, Beniamino Gigli, Giovanni Martinelli, and Ezio Pinza. Among the outstanding conductors was Arturo Toscanini, who later brilliantly directed the orchestra of the Philharmonic Symphony Society of New York. Italian opera singers and musicians performed regularly and with great success in Chicago, San Francisco, and other cities helping spread culture and appreciation for good music across the United States.

The Italian-language press addressed itself to people who had seldom (if ever) read newspapers, or anything else, for that matter, in the homeland. Papers published in Europe, as Robert Park has observed, were "not addressed to the common man."[21] Language in the immigrant papers was simple, direct, phonetic. Americanized and slang versions of the mother tongue appeared frequently. The papers that survived longest generally lost their European appearance and style in order to imitate the style and format of successful American dailies, with illustrations, headlines, and bizarre or dramatic stories. The ethnic press served as a bridge between life in the European village and that in the American city, providing identifiable leadership for the immigrant community and voicing group demands and complaints. Italian-language journals eased the first critical years of immigrant adjustment to the United States. As the immigrant generation moved into the American community or died out, the need for ethnic-language papers declined, and the journals disappeared, combined, or were changed into monthly publications.

The first important Italian-language newspaper in the United States was *L'Eco d'Italia*, printed weekly in New York City. It was founded in 1849 by G. F. Secchi de Casali, an able and talented journalist, a social reformer, and a leader in the city's predominantly Northern Italian community. San Francisco's large and prosperous Italian colony early supported *L'Eco della Patria*, established in 1859 as a semiweekly, and it appears to have been the first Italian paper to recognize the value of advertising as a means of financial support. The paper lasted until 1872, when it was absorbed by *La Voce del Popolo*, which had been in existence since December 1867.

After 1880, Italian colonies in American cities expanded rapidly in size as ever-increasing numbers of immigrants arrived. While the second generation quickly turned away from things foreign—that is, Italian—the rapidly growing numbers of first-generation immigrants made journalistic ventures more attractive. In Chicago alone at least twenty Italian-language newspapers appeared during the years between 1880 and 1921, when restrictive legislation stopped the flow of free immigration. The most popular and influential papers were *L'Italia* and *La Tribuna Italiana Transatlantica*, founded in 1886 and 1898 respectively. By 1921 *L'Italia* boasted more than 38,000 subscribers, while *La Tribuna's* circulation totaled 25,000. The country's leading Italian-language newspaper was *Il Progresso Italo-Americano* of New York City. Founded in 1880 by former padrone Carlo Barsotti, *Il Progresso* soon expanded its influence and readership far beyond New York, and by 1921 had a daily circulation of 110,000. Subscribers were located in all parts of the country although the majority resided in or near New York City.

Strangely, considering the great success he achieved with *Il Progresso*, Barsotti did not found his newspaper either for business or for philanthropic reasons but out of pique. In Barsotti's opinion the editor of *L'Eco d'Italia*, the only Italian-language newspaper then being published in New York, did not pay enough attention to Barsotti's communications concerning the fate of an Italian immigrant in the city condemned to death for murdering his wife. From his anger and irritation came the determination to start a rival newspaper. Although a novice in the field of journalism, the Tuscan-born Barsotti was a shrewd businessman who by the turn of the century had transformed a minor venture in a completely

Table 8. Number of Italian-Language Newspapers
Published in the United States, 1884–1920

1884 – 7	1893 –⎫ 15	1902 – 39	1911 – 73
1885 – 6	1894 –⎬	1903 – 42	1912 – 77
1886 – 5	1895 – 17	1904 – 46	1913 – 84
1887 – 7	1896 – 24	1905 – 57	1914 – 86
1888 – 9	1897 – 29	1906 – 63	1915 – 96
1889 – 12	1898 – 29	1907 – 71	1916 – 93
1890 – 11	1899 – 36	1908 – 76	1917 – 103
1891 – 13	1900 – 35	1909 – 75	1918 – 110
1892 – 14	1901 – 36	1910 – 73	1919 – 103
			1920 – 98

Based on Robert E. Park, *The Immigrant Press and Its Control* (New York 1922), facing p. 318.

new field of activity into the most successful and influential Italian-language newspaper in the United States. In fact, the paper had "the largest circulation of any foreign-language daily in the United States with the exception of the Jewish *Forward*."[22]

Small in circulation but influential in their particular spheres were radical papers such as *La Parola dei Socialisti*, begun in Chicago in 1908, and newspapers published by religious groups. Among the latter was *La Fiaccola* founded in 1898 by the Methodist Book Concern in New York City. Both radical and religious journals were designed for—and reached—nationwide audiences that were specialized but numerically limited.

The American press profoundly influenced its foreign-language counterparts with such innovations as large, bold headlines and brief articles, special features, photographs, and cartoons. Although successful Italian-language papers often started as journals written in the European style, they soon began to adopt American standards in content and appearance and featured sensational news stories—often reprinted directly from American newspapers. Unsuccessful papers generally did not adjust or did not last long

enough to adjust to American techniques. Like American newspapers, the Italian-language press also experienced the often disastrous effects of technological changes. New, expensive, and intri-
cate machinery, for example, required highly trained and hence
highly paid personnel. New equipment and higher labor costs
forced small and generally unremunerative papers of the pre-
World War I era to consolidate into larger units with greater pur-
chasing power.

Nearly all Italian-language periodicals faced another serious
shortage, that of competent reporters. Even writers for the more
successful papers supplemented meager salaries with money provided by the Italian consul, who subsidized journalists in order
to keep items favorable to Italy and appeals for remittances to the
homeland constantly before readers.

In addition to the lack of adequately trained personnel, relatively small circulations, insufficient funds to hire or train workers,
and limited prestige and authority, even more serious problems
beset Italian-language journals. They regularly lost readers as
the larger American environment absorbed immigrants. Second-
generation Italians cared very little about foreign-language papers.
In 1922 the Foreign-Language Information Service reported in its
monthly *Bulletin* not only that American-born children of immigrants preferred to read American papers, but also that the foreign-
born themselves "as soon as they have acquired sufficient English,
turn to the American papers for American and general news, depending on the press of their language for little more than news of
the home country."[23]

Italian-language papers were written in Americanized Italian,
and as the immigration, the source of readership, began to decline
in the 1920s so did the press. By the 1930s radio was successfully
competing with the press in the latter's role of providing news of
the homeland and of the local Italian community for the small
but steady stream of new immigrants to the United States. In
addition to news, radio provided dramatic playlets, humorous
sketches, and music. In fact, musical items—operatic arias and

overtures, and Italian popular and folk songs—absorbed approximately 70 percent of all Italian radio time.

Unlike the press and fraternal societies, the Church existed for newcomers before they left Europe. In Italy, the Church formed an integral part of life; in America, Italians found the Church to be a cold, remote, puritanical institution, controlled and often staffed, even in Italian neighborhoods, by the hated Irish. Devout Catholics and atheists alike resented Irish domination of the institution, demanded Italian priests, and sought to control the churches in their communities. Liberals and nationalists decried the Church's opposition to Italian unification and its refusal to recognize the Kingdom of Italy. By 1900 Italians appeared to be so dissatisfied that many Catholics believed there existed a serious threat to the Church's future in the United States.

Protestants seized the opportunity to seek converts. They publicly supported the Italian Kingdom and denounced papal intransigence. Some Protestant sects, especially Methodists, Baptists, and Presbyterians, worked actively among Italian immigrants in urban America. They supported 326 churches and missions and printed numerous newspapers, books, articles, pamphlets, and leaflets in Italian and English. Protestant settlements and missions, evangelizing social workers, public-school teachers, and ministers influenced some Italians to turn toward Protestantism. Despite costly and prodigious efforts by non-Catholic churches and settlement houses, however, relatively few Italians converted; those who did usually transferred to congregations in American neighborhoods.

Although most Italian immigrants remained nominally or actually loyal to Catholicism, their loyalty differed from that of other Catholic groups such as the Irish or Polish Americans. Jesuit Priest W. H. Agnew, in an article published in 1913, contrasted the religious attitudes of Italian newcomers with immigrants from Ireland and Poland and observed that "these latter came to America heroically attached to their religion, well instructed in it, faithful in the use of its Sacraments, and ready to die for it." Unlike the situation in Italy, the Church was so important to Irish and Polish peasants that, if necessary, they were ready to leave "home and country rather than live upon the reward of its denial."[24]

National consciousness, which developed among immigrant groups in the United States, strongly influenced ethnic attitudes toward religion. Irish and Polish nationalists considered Catholicism to be a central part of their nationalism; for Italians, Catholicism and nationalism exerted opposing forces.* Hence, at the same time that they raged against the Church both in Italy and the United States, Italian-American leaders urged compatriots to support the "Italian Church" against Irish "usurpers" and Protestants, and to "stand fast to the traditions of their fathers' religion."[25]

The image worship and simple superstitions that made religion a daily part of life to the unlettered immigrant seemed, to more sophisticated American critics, to indicate an irreligious or pagan attitude. In the same way, observers considered the Italian addiction to festivals, processions, and feasts to be a perversion of religion, although to participants such celebrations formed a basic part of worship and an extension of much-loved homeland traditions. What Americans saw as a falling-away from religion was partly an adaptation of old habits to new conditions, and partly an effort to counteract the Irish influence in the American Church.

In order to gain and hold the support of immigrants and their children, the Church in the United States found it necessary to offer a variety of services that were partly or entirely nontheological in nature, and which had been unnecessary in the static homeland village. These new facilities included missions, lay societies, and Sunday schools, and they formed part of a general movement in the American Catholic Church during the period between 1890 and World War I toward meeting the needs of immigrants. The

---

* At least until 1929. In that year the Vatican and the Italian government reached an agreement in the form of a treaty and Concordat by which the Church recognized the Kingdom's existence and the Italian occupation of Rome in exchange for acceptance of the sovereign status of Vatican City, indemnities, and recognition of Catholicism as the state religion.

most significant manifestation of the new concern among American Catholics appeared in the establishment of a number of national parishes served either by Italians or by Irish- and German-American priests who spoke Italian.

The Church intended national parishes to fulfill the needs of Italians and other non-English-speaking newcomers and to aid the immigrants to accommodate to their new homeland. In the ethnic parish, newcomers from different localities in Italy found that they had to forget or suppress Old World prejudices against outsiders (that is, anyone from another town or province) in order to form the desired national church.

Catholics expressed deep concern that most Italian parents sent their children to public rather than parochial schools. Italian-language papers tended to support and encourage Italian nonsupport of parochial education. Protestants, liberals, Italian nationalists, and socialists, attacked the entire concept of Catholic schools, which they viewed as a means through which the Church sought to establish mind control. They called upon Italians to send their children to public schools, arguing that religion should be taught in the home and not in school. For the average immigrant, however, economic considerations and availability rather than the fear of Church domination determined the decision to enroll youngsters in public schools.

Although each community institution or organization—press, mutual-aid society, Church, theater, immigrant bank, and labor agent—served vital functions during the early stages of immigrant adjustment, each, with one exception, declined to the advantage of an American counterpart. While the role of other institutions decreased as Italians and their children made use of American newspapers, insurance companies, banks, and trade unions (and in the process forsook foreign counterparts), the importance of the Catholic Church increased. In contrast to other immigrant agencies, the American equivalent to the national parish formed part of a larger institution, not a foreign and competing agency. The Catholic Church remained flexible enough to provide for the social and religious needs of new arrivals from overseas as well as long-time immigrant colony residents and inhabitants of middle-class outer city and suburban neighborhoods.

As immigrants and their children—after years of settlement in American cities—moved away from the ethnic colony and into American institutions, they found the Church to be the one organization that existed in the new neighborhood in much the same form as it had in the old locality. Their former (national) church had used the Italian language in sermons and confessions; priests in the new parish conducted these and other services in English. In both churches, the liturgy of the mass was in Latin, while rituals and vestments were as they always had been.

Identification with the colony, and use of its facilities and institutions, not only indicated a growth away from homeland outlook, but also formed for many newcomers a vital step in assimilation. Some immigrants ignored all community institutions and never expanded their loyalty or interest beyond their home village; even the Kingdom of Italy lay outside their comprehension. Some chose to make use of a few or all existing community institutions and gradually identified themselves with the "Italian" group, a concept that did not exist for them before their emigration; others saw immigrant churches, theaters, journals, and societies as intermediaries through which to learn American customs and ideas. Often members of this assimilation-oriented group arrived as children or young adults and absorbed (or consciously adopted) American habits and speech from the outside community—from schools, settlement houses, criminal gangs, and political organizations.

For all Italian immigrants the family filled basic needs and served important functions in the assimilation process. Whether newcomers used immigrant district institutions or those in the larger American environment or ignored them all, there was the family. The family was special. Like other institutions, however, the family also underwent change in the course of settlement in America.

CHAPTER 8

The Family in Italy and America

Immigrants and their descendants firmly believed that the Southern-Italian family* was re-created in the Little Italys of America. Actually the Old World family and community they remembered fondly was largely a myth. Thus one second-generation Italian-American leader in Chicago during the 1920s described his neighborhood as having "the same kind of warmth, friendliness, and intimacy in our community life that was to be found in the small towns of Sicily from whence our parents came."[1] Family "unity and strength" in Southern Italy and Sicily was, in actuality, more an ideal than an accomplished fact.

The land from which the immigrants came was largely pre-industrial and rural. Typical of such a society, the family comprised the core of Southern Italy's social structure and interpreted the outside world to family members. Interests and needs of the family influenced attitudes held toward Church, state, school, and other institutions. Sociologist Floyd Mansfield Martinson has noted that "there was intimate interplay of the [Southern Italian] peasant family with religious practices, the planting and gathering of food, the celebration of feasts and holidays, the education of the children, the treatment of sick, the protection of the person, and all other aspects of small-village folk life."[2] Luigi Barzini put it even

---

* See Chapter 2 for a discussion of the family in the context of Southern-Italian society.

more strongly. Within the walls and among the members of the family, Barzini wrote, "the individual finds consolation, help, advice, provisions, loans, weapons, allies and accomplices to aid him in his pursuits. No Italian who has a family is ever alone."[3] The immediate family, in the view of still another observer, comprised "the only people in the world you can really trust."[4] The individual in such a society was subordinate to group interests and needs. Each person was expected to protect the family's honor and to avenge any breach of that honor.

Within the immediate, or nuclear, family each member had his or her own special functions and responsibilities. The father, the interpreter of family needs and interests, held the highest status. He was highly authoritarian and a strict disciplinarian who ruled the home with a firm hand. No one in the family was allowed to undertake an enterprise without obtaining the father's permission, not even the eldest son who enjoyed a special status and was granted many privileges. The father customarily used verbal and physical punishment to control the behavior of offspring. Words of approval and expressions of affection, on the other hand, were doled out sparingly.

The father's control over the family was not unqualified. Instead, as Leonard Covello has demonstrated, it was contingent upon several factors. As long as the father was "the main provider, as long as he was healthy in mind and body, his rule and authority were unquestioned." Old age, debilitating illness, or mental disorder altered his status. His rule was also threatened if his wife died. As long as he remained a widower the father faced the threat of loss of his dominant role when a son, and it did not have to be the oldest, married. When that happened, the "widowed father surrendered the representation of the family to this son."[5]

Although subordinate to the father, the mother played a vital role in the family. The center of domestic life, she had a strong voice in important family decisions. The typical Southern-Italian family was large, and the mother exercised primary reponsibility both for raising the children and for mediating between them and the father. The mother's area of responsibility was the house. She cooked the food, bought or made all the clothes worn by her husband and children, selected wives for her sons, and managed whatever money resources the family possessed. The mother was expected not to venture far from the home and she was not to work for outsiders or for wages. The mother ruled the house but only at the direction of the husband. Even if he did not deserve it she obeyed his wishes. Southern-Italian attitudes toward wives were summed up in the saying: "Like a good weapon, she should be cared for properly; like a hat she should be kept straight; like a mule should be given plenty of work and occasional beatings. Above all, she should be kept in her place as a subordinate, for there is no peace in the house where a woman leads her husband."[6]

This was, at any rate, the male version of the ideal mate. It was not, however, reality. "Contrary to an assumed pattern," wives and mothers enjoyed a higher status than could be expected in a supposedly patriarchal society such as the Italian South. The wife's compliance was more in the nature of carrying out patterns of behavior than in an imbued or inculcated sense of submission. Although outwardly "the family organization was under the domination of the father," in practice the mother generally had "the last word" in important decisions. Thus in effect the Southern Italian father occupied "a pedestal of priority" while the real power, including control over the family's pursestrings, was in the wife's hands.[7]

The wife also enjoyed the respect and admiration of all family members. The father's control over the family was based solely and entirely on the fear inculcated in all family members. When the father weakened physically the fear decreased and eventually was replaced by a form of respect accorded those of advanced age. The mother, on the other hand, was an object of special respect and love. As the parents aged and the father's authority declined the prestige of the mother increased. As one Southern Italian put it, "I obey my mother's word, which is like the [word of] God."[8] But appearances and traditions must always be maintained. Thus, although the elderly wife's prestige grew at the expense of her husband's, she was careful to always play the part of the submissive female when in the presence of outsiders.

Parents expected respect and obedience from children, who assumed responsibilities at an early age. Families were large and the numerous children, especially the boys, were looked upon as economic assets. Not only did sons seek employment while still quite young, but most—if not all—of the wages earned were turned over to the parents. It was an accepted fact that all sons in a family had greater social value than did female children.

Daughters patterned themselves on their mothers in order to prepare themselves for marriage and motherhood. Formal schooling was not considered to be necessary or even desirable for girls. Instead, a daughter's education was based on participation in the activities of family life and "consisted of preparing her to carry out the duties as wife and mother in strict accordance with the familial code of behavior."[9] By the age of six or seven and sometimes even earlier a daughter was expected to set aside her games and rag dolls and turn her hand to useful work in the house or with her parents in the fields. She was expected to care for the younger children, help with the house cleaning, and take over a variety of chores, including the collection of fire wood and the drawing of water from the village well.

When the children were ready for marriage, usually by their early teens, they were expected to accept a mate chosen by the parents from among the youth of the same village. Romantic love or sexual attraction played little if any part in the selection of a mate. Marriage represented the union of two families as well as two individuals. Nevertheless, the basic social unit remained the nuclear family—that is, parents and unmarried children.

Once a child married, he or she helped to establish a new and separate economic and social unit. The idealized extended family —the clan of uncles, aunts, nephews, nieces, and cousins of varying degrees of closeness, working together harmoniously for the common good—existed only as an ideal. Harsh economic and social conditions forced each person to concentrate on the interests and needs of the immediate family. Envy, jealousy, and suspicion typified contacts with and attitudes toward all others, including the extended family. The following proverb underlined this reality of Southern-Italian life: "If you want a happy life, stay away from your relatives."

The man of the family turned to relatives only when he needed a favor, but because his own prestige increased in proportion to the loss of a relative's prestige, he acted prudently if he did not completely trust kinsmen. Thus, although in Southern-Italian villages most residents were related, there was little closeness, cohesiveness, or feeling of unity among the villagers. According to a priest from Calabria, "a 'neighbor' to the people in South Italy was one who lived next door. However one who was only two doors removed was merely a *paesano*."

A sense of community did not exist. A Tuscan officer on duty in Sicily was shocked by the complete absence, as far as he could observe, "of cooperation between the peasants. One would say they all hate each other." Such concepts as mankind, Italy, and responsibility for the needs of others were beyond the social grasp of the Southern peasant because for them the only real "world" was the family circle. Leonard Covello has noted that "it would be impossible to imagine the *contadino* in South Italy contributing toward the Italian Red Cross, or the Society for Aid to the Blind."[10] Cooperative efforts such as that represented by these organizations were, as sociologist Francis Ianni notes, simply too far removed from the usual concepts developed "within the narrow confines of family life" in the South. This attitude changed in the New World, where under the stress of life in a strange and alien environment, the extended family took on increased importance among the immigrants. Yet "even in America, the ideal of the closely knit, socially and economically integrated extended family remained illusory."[11]

Despite numerous pressures and influences in the American environment that would eventually bring changes in the Italian-

American family, the immigrants initially were successful in resist-
ing these forces. The traditional Italian family pattern remained
relatively intact during the first few years in the United States. This
stemmed in large part from the belief that the stay in America
would be brief and that the family would return to the familiar
patterns of life in the home village life.

If the family remained in the United States it eventually entered
what sociologist Paul Campisi has termed the "conflict" stage.
According to Campisi this generally began during the second
decade of living in America or "specifically, when the children
unhesitatingly express their acquired American expectations and
attempt to transmit them in the family situation and when the
parents in turn attempt to reinforce the pattern of the Old World
peasant family."[12] In the process the family became, in Francis
Ianni's words, "only fictitiously patriarchal." The father no longer
inspired awe. He was more likely to be loved than feared. In large
measure this was because the children, who spent long periods of
time out of the house each day, gained a degree of independence
undreamed of by their counterparts in Southern Italy, while such
functions as education, recreation, work, and religion which were
family-centered in the Italian village "were more and more fulfilled
by the American community."[13] The changes that took place,
however, generally were gradual and often proceeded unrecognized
by the family members themselves. This was evident in the experience of immigrants who, after some years of residence in the
United States, returned to Italy and expressed surprise and disap-
pointment that "the Old Country" had changed so much since they
left, not realizing that it was they and not the village of origin and
its people that had changed. In fact, the towns of Southern Italy
had remained virtually unchanged for hundreds of years. As one
immigrant reported in 1912 on his return from a visit to the be-
loved home village in Sicily, after eleven years of residence in
Brooklyn, "people there live in miserable little shacks. They don't
have nothing. That's not the way I remember it." Nevertheless,
that *is* the way things were in the homeland.

The process of settlement in the United States profoundly affected the family as well as other institutions. Within the typical immigrant family two cultures came into conflict, a recurring theme explored by Jerre Mangione in *Mount Allegro*, and by other novelists. Italian immigrant parents wanted to conduct family life according to Old World patterns, and attempted to establish relationships as they remembered them. The children, on the other hand, wanted to behave in what they considered to be "the American way." As the children learned English, whether in school or on the street, family roles and relationships began slowly to alter. The children rather than the parents understood the world in which they lived, or at least they thought they did. As a result the young gained a voice in family affairs. Dependence on the children was especially difficult for the father to accept, because it deposed him from his position of authority. Unlike the homeland where peasant-class youngsters existed for the benefit of their parents, at least until they married, immigrant children in America learned to live their own lives and to pursue their own interests and welfare. Gradually the children began to break away from parental control and to exert their individualism. The boys typically escaped into the streets to seek companionship and a sense of security in neighborhood youth gangs.

Particularly troublesome to immigrant parents was the altered role of daughters. Sons had traditionally been allowed some freedom of action, befitting their future role as heads of families. Expected, in the old country, to prepare for wifehood and motherhood, daughters in America grew into new roles largely because of economic necessity. The family usually had to send as many members out to work as possible in order to increase income. Thus wives and daughters, as well as sons, took jobs.

Careful study of documentary material for 1896 and 1911 led historian Elizabeth Pleck to conclude that "Italian wives were as likely to work as German or Irish wives and more often employed than Polish or Russian Jewish married women . . . Nor did Italian traditionalism prevent daughters from working in American

Table 9. Differences Between the Southern Italian Peasant Family in Italy and the First- and Second-Generation Italian Family in America

Southern Italian Peasant Family in Italy	First-Generation Southern Italian Family in America	Second-Generation Southern Italian Family in America
A. *General characteristics:*		
1. Patriarchal	Fictitiously patriarchal	Tends to be democratic
2. Folk-peasant	Quasi-urban	Urban and modern
3. Well integrated	Disorganized and in conflict	Variable, depending on the particular family situation
4. Stationary	Mobile	High degree of mobility
5. Active community life	Inactive in the American community but somewhat active in the Italian neighborhood	Inactive in the Italian neighborhood, but increasingly active in American community
6. Emphasis on the sacred	Emphasis on the sacred is weakened	Emphasis on the secular
7. Home and land owned by family	In the small city the home may be owned, but in a large city the home is usually a flat or an apartment	Ownership of home is an ideal, but many are satisfied with flat
8. Strong family and community culture	Family culture in conflict	Weakened family culture reflecting vague American situation
9. Sharing of common goals	No sharing of common goals	No sharing of common goals
10. Children live for the parents	Children live for themselves	Parents live for the children
11. Children are an economic asset	Children are an economic asset for few working years only and may be an economic liability	Children are an economic liability
12. Many family celebrations of special feasts, holidays, etc.	Few family celebrations of feasts and holidays	Christmas only family affair, with Thanksgiving being variable
13. Culture is transmitted only by the family	Italian culture is transmitted only by family, but American culture is transmitted by	American culture is transmitted by the family and by other American institutions

Table 9. (*continued*)

Southern Italian Peasant Family in Italy	First-Generation Southern Italian Family in America	Second-Generation Southern Italian Family in America
A. General characteristics:	American institutions other than the family	
14. Strong in-group solidarity	Weakened in-group solidarity	Little in-group solidarity
15. Many functions: economic, recreational, religious, social, affectional, and protective	Functions include semi-recreational, social, and affectional	Functions reduced to affectional, in the main
B. Size:		
1. Large-family system	Believe in a large-family system but cannot achieve it because of migration	Small-family system
2. Many children (10 is not unusual)	Fair number of children (10 is unusual)	Few children (10 is rare)
3. Extended kinship to godparents	Extended kinship, but godparent relationship is weakened	No extended kinship to godparents
C. Roles and statuses:		
1. Father has highest status	Father loses high status, or it is fictitiously maintained	Father shares high status with mother and children; slight patriarchal survival
2. Primogeniture: eldest son has high status	Rule of primogeniture is variable; success more important than position	No primogeniture; all children tend to have equal status
3. Mother center of domestic life only and must not work for wages	Mother center of domestic life but may work for wages and belong to some clubs	Mother acknowledges domestic duties but reserves time for much social life and may work for wages
4. Father can punish children severely	Father has learned that American law forbids this	Father has learned it is poor psychology to do so
5. Family regards	Family does not have	Family struggles for

Table 9. (*continued*)

Southern Italian Peasant Family in Italy	First-Generation Southern Italian Family in America	Second-Generation Southern Italian Family in America
C. *Roles and statuses:*		
itself as having high status and role in the community	high status and role in the American community but may have it in the Italian colony	high status and role in the American community and tends to reject high status and role in the Italian community
6. Women are educated for marriage only	Women receive some formal education as well as family education for marriage	Emphasis is on general education with reference to personality development rather than to future marriage
7. The individual is subordinate to the family	Rights of the individual increasingly recognized	The family is subordinate to the individual
8. Daughter-in-law is subservient to the husband's family	Daughter-in-law is in conflict with husband's family	Daughter-in-law is more or less independent of husband's family
9. Son is expected to work hard and contribute to family income	Son is expected to work hard and contribute to family income, but this is a seldom-realized goal	Son expected to do well in school and need not contribute to family income
D. *Interpersonal relations:*		
1. Husband and wife must not show affection in the family or in public	Husband and wife are not demonstrative in public or in the family but tolerate it in their married children	Husband and wife may be demonstrative in the family and in public
2. Boys are superior to girls	Boys are regarded as superior to girls	Boys tend to be regarded as superior to girls, but girls have high status also
3. Father is consciously feared, respected, and imitated	Father is not consciously feared or imitated but is respected	Father is not consciously feared. He may be imitated and may be admired

Table 9. (*continued*)

Southern Italian Peasant Family in Italy	First-Generation Southern Italian Family in America	Second-Generation Southern Italian Family in America
D. *Interpersonal relations:*		
4. Great love for mother	Great love for mother but much ambivalence from cultural tensions	Love for mother is shared with father
5. Baby indulgently treated by all	Baby indulgently treated by all	Baby indulgently treated by all with increasing concern regarding sanitation, discipline, and sibling rivalry
E. *Marriage:*		
1. Marriage in early teens	Marriage in late teens or early twenties	Marriage in early or middle twenties
2. Selection of mate by parents	Selection of mate by individual with parental consent	Selection of mate by individual regardless of parental consent
3. Must marry someone from the same village	This is an ideal, but marriage with someone from same region (i.e., province) is tolerated; very reluctant permission granted to marry outside nationality; no permission for marriage outside religion	Increasing number of marriages outside nationality and outside religion
4. Dowry rights	No dowry	No dowry
5. Marriage always involves a religious ceremony	Marriage almost always involves both a religious and a secular ceremony	Marriage usually involves both, but there is an increasing number of marriages without benefit of religious ceremony
F. *Birth and child care:*		
1. Many magical and superstitious beliefs in connection with pregnancy	Many survivals of old beliefs and superstitions	Few magical and superstitious notions in connection with pregnancy

Table 9. (*continued*)

Southern Italian Peasant Family in Italy	First Generation Southern Italian Family in America	Second-Generation Southern Italian Family in America
F. *Birth and child care:*		
2. Delivery takes place in a special confinement room in the home; midwife assists	Delivery takes place generally in a hospital; may take place in home; family doctor displaces midwife	Delivery takes place almost always in a hospital; specialist, obstetrician, or general practitioner assists
3. Child illnesses are treated by folk remedies; local physician only in emergencies or crises	Child illnesses are treated partially by folk remedies but mostly by the family doctor	Child illnesses are treated by a pediatrician; much use of latest developments in medicine (vaccines, etc.)
4. Child is breast-fed either by the mother or by a wet nurse; weaning takes place at about end of 2d or 3d year by camouflaging the breasts	Child is breast-fed if possible; if not, it is bottle-fed; same practice with variations regarding weaning	Child is bottle-fed as soon as possible; breast-feeding is rare; no weaning problems
5. No birth control	Some birth control	Birth control is the rule
G. *Sex attitudes:*		
1. Child is allowed to go naked about the house up to the age of 5 or 6; after this there is rigid enforcement of the rule of modesty	Variable, depending on the individual family's situation	This is variable, depending on the individual family; development of modesty is much earlier than in Old World peasant family
2. Sex matters are not discussed in family	Sex matters are not discussed in family	Sex matters increasingly discussed in family but not as freely as in "old" American family
3. Adultery is severely punished by the man's	Adultery results in divorce or separation	Adultery may result in divorce or separation

Table 9. (*continued*)

Southern Italian Peasant Family in Italy	First Generation Southern Italian Family in America	Second-Generation Southern Italian Family in America
G. *Sex attitudes:* taking matters into his own hands		
4. Chastity rule rigidly enforced by chaperonage; lack of it grounds for immediate separation at wedding night	Attempts to chaperon fail, but chastity is an expectation; lack of it is grounds for separation, but there are few cases of this kind in America	No chaperonage; chastity is expected, but lack of it may be reluctantly tolerated
5. No premarital kissing and petting are allowed	No premarital kissing and petting are allowed openly	Premarital kissing and petting are allowed openly
6. Boys and girls attend separate schools	Schools are coeducational	Schools are coeducational
H. *Divorce and separation:*		
1. No divorce allowed	No divorce allowed, but some do divorce	Religion forbids it, but it is practiced
2. Desertion is rare	Desertion is rare	Desertion is rare
I. *Psychological aspects:*		
1. Fosters security in the individual	Fostered conflict in the individual	Fosters security with some conflict lags
2. The family provides a specific way of life; hence, there is little personal disorganization	Family is in conflict, hence cannot provide a specific way of life; yields marginal American-Italian way of life	Family reflects confused American situation, does not give individual a specific way of life, but marginality is weakened
3. Recreation is within family	Recreation is both within and outside the family	Recreation is in the main outside the family; this is variable, depending on individual family situation

Paul Campisi, "Ethnic Family Patterns: The Italian Family in the United States," *American Journal of Sociology*, **LIII** (May 1948), 444–46.

sweatshops and factories, generally with parental approval."[14]

A survey of working women in New York City published in 1919 found that 91 percent of the daughters fourteen years of age and older in Italian families worked for wages. When a girl became a wage earner, she gained a sense of independence completely alien to her counterparts in Southern Italy. One New York Italian colony girl summed up the problem unmarried women in the United States faced: "Our parents think you can just sit home and wait for a man to come asking for your hand—like a small town in Italy. They don't realize that here a girl has got to get out and do something about it."[15] Courtship patterns emerged that were a mixture of rural-Italian and urban-American dating customs.

The majority of the Southern-Italian immigrants in the United States were between eighteen and forty-five years of age. Most married and raised families in the new homeland. Marriage generally took place in the late teens or early twenties, a later age than was generally the case in Italy. Another change from Old World behavior was that although parental consent was sought, offspring demanded the right to have a voice in choosing their mate and to base their decision on the principle of romantic love. This was true even of the girls. As social worker Ida L. Hull observed, in a speech presented before the National Conference of Social Work in 1924, the Italian girl brought up in America "is apt to rebel. She insists on having some part in choosing a husband for herself, perhaps by the elimination of several admirers before she picks out the most favored one."[16]

Immigrant youngsters generally married within the Italian group although increasingly they chose mates from outside the village or province of family origin. Among the second, or American generation, which included those who arrived as infants or children as well as those born in the United States, marriage increasingly took place with non-Italians and even with non-Catholics. This innovation was especially typical of the upwardly mobile. Studies conducted at least as early as 1916 noted a tendency on the part of upwardly mobile young Italian men "to marry girls of other nationalities whom they meet in the freer contacts of American life."[17] Doctors, lawyers, and other professionals, merchants, politicians, policemen and others in public employment, and even some criminals married Irish, German, Jewish, Scandinavian, or Anglo-Saxon women. Because of their more sheltered upbringing, girls generally did not meet as many outsiders as did male family members, but as they found employment among non-Italians their range of choices also expanded. Nevertheless, during the twenties and thirties the majority of the American generation selected marriage partners from within the Italian group but generally on their own terms rather than those imposed by parents. For second-generation girls, as well as for young men, this was an almost inevitable result of the situation that "every American institution and every influence" with which she came in contact conspired to loosen the bonds of Old World custom and tradition and "transfer responsibility from parents to the girl herself."[18]

Members of the second generation generally either directly challenged parental control over the process of courtship or, more typically, they resorted to subterfuge. Thus, according to sociologist Michael Lalli, "dates were not specifically arranged. Young men and girls would make their appearance as members of separate groups knowing well exactly who would be there" when school events, public dances, or picnics were scheduled. Although such meetings, Lalli notes, were ostensibly " 'accidental,' a young man would often have the opportunity of taking a girl home. If the relationship developed to the point where a date or two was arranged in advance and the young man called at the girl's home—there was a strong presumption in the Italian community that an engagement announcement would soon be made."[19]

Changes were also evident in parental attitudes toward education. In Southern Italy education was considered to be a privilege reserved for the landowning class. Nathan Glazer and Daniel Patrick Moynihan have accurately noted that "education was for a cultural style of life and professions the peasant could never aspire to. Nor was there an ideology of change; intellectual curiosity and originality were ridiculed or suppressed." An old Southern-Italian proverb reflected another concern: "Do not make your child better than you are."[20] This obviously was not the middle-class ideal presented and emphasized in urban-American public schools which Italian-immigrant and second-generation youngsters attended. Nor was it the message communicated in classes offered by settlement houses.

Italian immigrants won notoriety (and the wrath of social workers and other concerned Americans) for denying their children adequate schooling; while complaining that their own lack of education kept them from getting better jobs, parents sent their offspring out to work in order to supplement family incomes.

According to statistics collected by the United States Immigration Commission for the period from 1899 to 1910, Southern Italians had among the highest illiteracy rate of all the Southern- and Eastern-European groups. Southern-Italian immigrants fourteen years of age or over totaled 1,690,376, of whom 911,566 (or 53.9 percent) were illiterate. Of the smaller Northern-Italian contingent, 11.5 percent (or 38,897) of a total immigration of

Table 10. Nationality of Parents Charged with Violation of Compulsory Education Law, January–July 1908

Native American	207
Italian	270
Russian	66
German	56
Irish	55
Polish	29
English	7
Others	22
Total	712

New York City Department of Education, *Annual Report of the City Superintendent of Schools*, 1907–8, p. 356.

339,301 were illiterate. Only Turks and Portuguese exceeded the Southern-Italian figures. The East-European Jewish rate was 26 percent (209,507 illiterates in a total immigration of 806,786). Although most Italians eventually complied with the minimum requirements of compulsory-education laws, they secured jobs for their children after school hours. While compulsory-education laws required school attendance until the age of sixteen, early departure at age fourteen was permitted if the youth obtained a work permit. The recency of the Southern-Italian immigration is reflected in the fact that although less than one percent of Italian youngsters in the years prior to World War I were enrolled in high school, 72.7 percent were in the primary grades. Another reason for the small proportion of high school students should be noted: because of economic necessity, Italian youngsters were withdrawn from school at the first opportunity and put to work.

Some parents preferred their children to attend parochial schools where they would receive religious training and learn to read and write Italian, a language not widely taught in public school. Many of those immigrants who felt concern over the religious and language training of their children balked at paying the tuition required by private schools. An Italian parent who believed that his children ought to contribute financially to the family's welfare would not look with favor on paying for the schooling acquired by his offspring, for this represented a double loss of money. Parochial schools were, however, often used by parents whose boys or girls were disciplinary problems. These children were withdrawn from public schools and sent to religious institutions in the hope that the sisters would be more successful in controlling them.

The problem of truancy and child labor involved more than a desire (spurred by necessity) to put all family members to work in order to survive the scramble for existence that characterized the slums. An additional factor, the cultural problem of adapting to new life patterns, resulted from the movement from rural surroundings to an urban environment. The conflict between immediate financial gain and long-range educational advantage was common to all newcomers who struggled to make the most of their new urban opportunities. Foreign-born children, including Italians, often left school because of unpleasant classroom experiences. To a newly arrived immigrant child or a youngster whose family spoke English poorly or not at all, school could be a frightening world.

In time many immigrants came to recognize the value of education. They took advantage of adult-education programs offered at settlement houses, the Young Men's Christian Association, and public schools. Others used the opportunities presented by adult-education classes to compensate for the inadequate schooling forced upon them by economic necessity and other personal factors; while many who arrived as uneducated adults found in American public-school evening classes a chance to make up for their lack of training.

That Italian immigrants appreciated the importance of education was shown in the attitudes of those who returned to Europe. Homeland Italians found concern over education and efforts to improve schools to be a major distinguishing characteristic of those who had lived in America. For those who remained in the United States and for their children, increased interest in education made it possible for many to enter commercial, trade, or professional classes. One authority observed in 1921 that along with immigrant community institutions, the public school ranked of vital importance in aiding the newcomer "to find his place and make his way in America."[21]

Social-settlement houses located in Italian and other core-area ethnic neighborhoods offered a wide variety of activities and services utilized by numerous immigrants and their children. Settlements generally maintained social, civic, political, domestic, musical, athletic, and dramatic clubs for adults and provided lessons in English and citizenship for the foreign-born. They also offered music lessons, gymnastic facilities, arts and crafts classes, concerts, lectures, and forums. Lighter entertainment included festivals, pageants, and dances. Many settlements kept libraries and study rooms available. Some, including all the larger establishments, maintained playgrounds, camps, and vacation houses and took members on summer outings. These activities usually won steady, if not overwhelming, immigrant support and participation and aided substantially in their adjustment and that of the second generation.

When the American generation grew to maturity and married three main family types evolved. One involved the complete abandonment of the Old World way of life in favor of American ideas and patterns of behavior. The objective was to adjust, or become like Americans, in as short a period of time as possible. This adjustment included movement from the Italian neighborhood, abandonment of the Italian language for exclusive use of English, and, in many instances, change of the family name to an American-sounding one. This group constituted a minority of the second generation—at most, a quarter of the total—and was comprised of the better-educated and ambitious, including businessmen, professionals, and white-collar employees.

Another type of second-generation family tended to perpetuate Old World patterns. According to Paul Campisi, the family's "interaction with the non-Italian world is at a minimum, and its interests are tied up with those of the Italian community."[22] Members remained in working-class occupations and lived in the Italian neighborhood close to the parental home. This element, easily identifiable, was generally assumed by ethnic community members as well as by outsiders to contain the majority of Italian Americans; in actuality it constituted a minority group.

The majority of second-generation Italian families attempted to adjust to American ways, but not so completely as to repudiate all parental ties. The family generally moved away from the Italian district and over the years reduced contacts with friends and acquaintances from "the old neighborhood." Communication with the parental household was, however, maintained and "relationships with the parents as well as with immigrant relatives are affectionate and understanding."[23] For the second generation the extended family apparently took on a greater importance than it had in the immigrant generation. It tended to become larger in size and "to be characterized by closer and more extensive social ties."[24]

Although some Italian words and phrases were known and used, the typical second-generation member was unable to communicate effectively in Italian. Despite parental pressures to produce numerous grandchildren, couples tended to have smaller families. Most of the families in this group came from the lower-middle and working classes. Although the structure of the family remained essentially patriarchal, the husband was less rigidly authoritarian than his father and more tolerant in his relations with his children. The wife became less submissive to, and less dependent upon, her husband than had been the case in her mother's generation. She obtained more education that had been permitted in the past and often found employment in the larger American community. Daughters had higher status than in earlier generations and enjoyed greater freedom.

Whether the children were boys or girls, the parents lived for them and were concerned about the welfare and happiness of the youngsters, unlike the typical Southern Italian, or even the immigrant family. Parents no longer selected marriage partners without regard for the interests or feelings of the offspring; in fact, individuals often selected their own mates, regardless of parental opinion. In general, the family was subordinated to the interests and needs of individual members.

By the 1940s the second-generation Italian family had oriented itself "increasingly toward an American way of Life." Thus Campisi could observe in 1948 that it had come to resemble "the contemporary American family."[25] The evolution of the Italian-American family resulted, at least in part, from the effects of federal legislation enacted during and after World War I to slow the flow of Italian and other European immigration to a trickle.

PART III

FROM IMMIGRANT TO ETHNIC

CHAPTER 9

The Interwar Years

World War I (1914–18) profoundly affected immigration and immigrant colonies in America. Manpower needs in the belligerent countries of Europe and the extreme difficulties of ocean passage during wartime cut sharply into the number of newcomers arriving from overseas. Italian immigration declined precipitously from 283,738 in 1914 to 49,688 in 1915 (the first full year of war) and all the way down to 5,250 in 1918. The virtual cessation of immigration ended the constant replenishment of labor reserves in the United States. Combined with military manpower demands in the period after the United States entered the war in April 1917 (in the United States Army alone were an estimated 300,000 Italian Americans, including 89,662 immigrants), labor shortages offered immigrants already in the country and their children wider job opportunities than ever before and at higher wages.

With the passage of legislation in 1917, 1921, and 1924 the United States reversed its traditional policy of free immigration. Social workers and other liberal elements among the American population joined Italians and other urban ethnics (under the guidance of Jewish organizations) in the fight against immigration restriction; but the outcome was never in doubt when business groups aligned themselves with organized labor in support of restriction. Organized labor traditionally supported the passage of federal legislation to restrict immigration in the belief that the constant stream of unskilled labor undermined unionizing efforts. During the war years, with traditional overseas sources of unskilled labor cut off, American industry discovered the availability of alternate sources of manpower. Migrations of Mexicans and of blacks from the American South removed industry's need for European immigrants. This development, along with such emotional factors as antiradicalism, religious bias, and racism, brought about the closing of America's "Golden Door" and the adoption of clearly discriminatory quota laws. The Immigration Act of 1924 (the Johnson-Reed Act) "reflecting racist warnings about a threat to the 'Anglo-Saxon' stock, aimed at freezing the country ethnically by sharply restricting the 'new' immigration from southern and eastern Europe."[1] Under the provisions of the Johnson-Reed Act a maximum yearly quota of 150,000 immigrants a year was admitted to the United States. The quota was based on country of origin. Italians were assigned a yearly quota of 3,845.

Although not leaders in the radical movement, two Italian immigrants, Nicola Sacco and Bartolomeo Vanzetti, personified to Americans the twin dangers of immigration and radicalism during the Red Scare hysteria following World War I which aided the efforts of restrictionists. Sacco and Vanzetti had been draft dodgers during World War I and were avowed anarchists. Sacco worked in a shoe factory while Vanzetti was a fish peddler. Both were active in Italian-colony working-class organizations. In May 1920 the two men were accused of the April 15, 1920, robbery and murder of the paymaster of a shoe factory and his guard in South Braintree, Massachusetts, as well as of an unsuccessful attempt to rob a payroll truck in downtown Bridgewater, Massachusetts, on the day before Christmas 1919. The men denied involvement in either holdup but were not believed by authorities. Vanzetti was put on trial at Plymouth, Massachusetts, in June 1920 for the attempted robbery. Although the evidence against him appeared to be weak Vanzetti was found guilty and sentenced to twelve to fifteen years in prison.

The trial began for both Sacco and Vanzetti in the South Braintree murder case on May 31, 1921, in Dedham, Massachusetts. After a month and a half of testimony the jury, on July 14, found the two men guilty of murder in the first degree. Supporters of the convicted men believed the decision was based on their foreign birth and political beliefs rather than on the evidence, which was circumstantial. The judge in the case, Webster Thayer, a Boston patrician, publicly expressed his contempt for anarchism and was alleged to have boasted to a friend at a football game in 1924: "Did you see what I did with those anarchistic bastards the other day? I guess that will hold them for a while."[2] During trial proceedings Thayer also permitted the prosecuting attorney, Frederick Katzmann, to make the defendants' radicalism a cornerstone of his case. While Katzmann effectively built the prosecution case Fred H. Moore, the chief counsel for the defense, complicated his clients' already serious problem. "Himself a radical and a professional defender of radicals," Moore was brilliant and hard-working but also quarrelsome and emotional, a combination of factors bound to cause friction with Judge Thayer. In addition, Moore, who was totally unfamiliar with the traditions of the Massachusetts bench and was not even a member of the state's bar, "found neither professional nor personal sympathies between himself and the Judge."[3] In 1948 Edmund Morgan, an authority on the law of evidence, cogently summarized the conduct of the trial: "Against a masterful and none too scrupulous prosecution was opposed a hopelessly mismanaged defense before a stupid trial judge."[4]

The case quickly assumed national and international significance. After numerous delays and despite the pleas of intellectuals, liberals, humanitarians, and other concerned Americans, Sacco and Vanzetti were executed on August 23, 1927. Supporters of the two men never lost hope that they would be exonerated. Finally, in 1977, Massachusetts Governor Michael Dukakis declared August 23 the fiftieth anniversary of the execution and stated that the trial leading to that execution had been unfair.

"It was one of the ironies of history," Lawrence Pisani observed in 1957, that "so soon after being charged with leftist tendencies," in the infamous Sacco-Vanzetti affair, Italian Americans "had to defend themselves against charges of attempting to introduce Fascism into the United States."[5] Events in the homeland attracted the attention and the admiration of many in the Italian-American community during the 1920s. Throughout the decade, Italian community residents exhibited an overriding concern for the homeland and its new experiment in government. The foreign-language press found Fascist dictator Benito Mussolini to be an ever-popular topic. Catholics approved of Il Duce's efforts to bridge the chasm that had existed between the Vatican and the Italian government since the creation of United Italy in 1861. The reconciliation of February 11, 1929, in the form of a treaty and Concordat by which the Church recognized the Kingdom's existence and occupation of Rome in exchange for acceptance of the sovereign status of Vatican City, indemnities, and recognition of Catholicism as the state religion, met with wild enthusiasm among Italians in the United States.

Although middle-class Italian Americans and members of the working class differed in many respects, their views coincided with regard to Mussolini: both groups heartily endorsed him. Il Duce won immense popularity because he seemed to be dealing effectively with homeland problems (such as Church-State relations, the Mafia, and radicalism). He thus provided, they felt, the ideal government for Italy. Upwardly mobile Italian Americans desired respect and acceptance from the native community, but realized that many Americans viewed them with contempt. They supported and glorified Italy in large part to win American admiration for Italian contributions to civilization. Suburbanites and residents of middle-class city neighborhoods as well as Italians living in tenement districts took pride in Italy's increased international status under Mussolini, and magnified Italy's achievements as a defense against American derision for "new" immigrant groups.

Thus Mussolini's basic importance to Italian Americans centered in their hope of being accepted as Americans. No longer was it necessary to point to dead heroes and vanished glories, for Italy now exhibited a swashbuckling leader who received the admiration and respect of many Americans and Englishmen, at least during the 1920s. For example, Nicholas Murray Butler, president of Columbia University and a recipient of the Nobel Peace Prize, found Fascism "a form of government of the very first order of excellence"; while Otto H. Kahn, head of a great American banking house, proclaimed in 1923 that "not only his own country but the world at large owes a debt of gratitude" to Benito Mussolini. In 1927 Winston Churchill, who in World War II would lead the British nation against Fascist Italy and Nazi Germany, stated, "If I were an Italian, I would don the Fascist Black Shirt."[6]

In the following decade American and English enthusiasm waned as the repressive aspects of the Fascist system became more apparent. A group of distinguished exiles who arrived in the 1930s attested to the shortcomings of a government that repelled and expelled its nation's finest minds. Among these were musician Arturo Toscanini, historians Gaetano Salvemini and Giuseppe Borgese, former Italian foreign minister Carlo Sforza, political scientist Mario Einaudi, virologist Salvador Luria, journalist Max Ascoli, literary historian Renato Poggioli, and physicists Enrico Fermi, Emilio Segre, and Bruno Rossi. Laura Fermi, who accompanied her husband Enrico to the New World in 1939, believes that "America proved once more a land of opportunity and a haven to which the persecuted of the world might continue to look with confidence. America did not ask a price for her services, but has been repaid in full from the intellectual migration in a currency compounded of prestige, knowledge, and a general enrichment of culture."[7]

The thirties formed a period of conflict within Italian-American communities between supporters and opponents of Fascism. The struggle took place in the press, in Italian-language radio broadcasts, in the meetings of Italian organizations, and occasionally on the streets. One such clash took place on Memorial Day 1927 in New York between parading groups of Fascists and anti-Facists. Two Fascists were killed and scores on each side were injured. There were also numerous instances over the years of the destruction of printing presses of one group or the other which immediately resulted in the smashing of the opposing group's presses.

Perhaps the most prominent and persistent anti-Fascist leader in America was the anarchist editor and activist Carlo Tresca. The Italian-born Tresca played a prominent role in the I.W.W.-led strikes in Lawrence, Massachusetts, and Patterson, New Jersey, in the years before World War I. Editor of radical newspapers since 1904 when he directed the fortunes of *Il Proletario* in Philadelphia, Tresca, during the 1920s, became owner, editor, and principal writer of the New York anarchist weekly paper *Il Martello* (The Hammer). Tresca was the object of Fascist violence throughout the thirties. Although several earlier attempts on his life failed, on January 11, 1943, Tresca's luck finally ran out. As he left his office after a long day of work a man walked up behind the editor and fired shots into Tresca's head and back. The sixty-year-old radical leader died on the sidewalk. It is not certain, however, that Fascists were responsible for the murder. Tresca abhorred and struggled as ardently against Russian Communism as he did Italian and German Fascism. American exponents of all of these ideologies were equally anxious to see the muckraking editor killed. Complicating the situation even more, the trouble-prone Tresca apparently also antagonized New York crime syndicate leaders. Although two men were arrested for the murder no one has ever been indicted. It appears that it will never be known who committed the crime or for what specific reason.

Tresca, Arturo Giovannitti, and other radical labor leaders of the pre-World War I era concentrated their attention on Fascism during the twenties only in part because of the threat to individual freedom posed by totalitarian Fascism. They also realized that because of the unparalleled prosperity of the decade their influence among the laboring masses, which even during the worst of economic times in the years before the First World War was limited, was now all but nonexistent.

The general prosperity that began during World War I and continued until late 1929 (except for the recession of 1920–21) facilitated the upward social and economic movement of Italians and members of other "new" immigrant groups. Their improved economic status brought greater self-esteem to the Italian community. During the twenties the increased affluence of many immigrants made possible, even speeded, the dispersion of Italians throughout all parts of American cities and their suburbs.

Along with the passage of legislation restricting further immigration, residential mobility greatly decreased ethnic community populations and lessened their importance. Upwardly mobile Italians emulated other urbanites when the opportunity presented itself of moving from core-area colonies to neighborhoods in the periphery of the city as well as into nearby suburbs. Although Italians had settled in industrial suburbs—so-called "satellite cities"—at least as early as the 1890s, the migration to middle- and upper-income suburbs of large cities did not begin until after World War I. This migration resulted from the prosperity of the 1920s. During the decade New York City Italians fanned out into the far reaches of Long Island and prosperous Westchester County while, in the Middle West, Italians by 1929 resided in every suburb of the Chicago metropolitan area. In San Francisco, Deanna Gumina relates, Italians by the 1920s "had gained sufficient social mobility to have married spouses of non-Italian descent, and they generally lived in Waspish districts of the city such as St. Francis Woods and Pacific Heights."[8]

For most Italians economic gains enjoyed during the twenties were modest; but to the individuals concerned, advances were significant. A comparison of occupations in New York City in 1916 and 1931 showed Italians moving away from employment as unskilled laborers. Although 50 percent worked as laborers in 1916, only 31 percent were still in this occupational category just fifteen years later. By 1931 Italians were found in increasing numbers as chauffeurs, clerks, mechanics, carpenters, salesmen, painters, and plasterers. Upwardly mobile Italians in the city generally found opportunities in the construction and consumer trades or as small proprietors. One source noted in the late thirties, however, that "every trade, business, and profession has its representatives among the Italians."[9] Most professional men still came either from the small Northern-Italian element or from the small portion of the Southern-Italian group that was of nonpeasant background. The largely Northern-Italian San Francisco group enjoyed outstanding success in business, especially in banking, during the interwar decades. The degree of achievement enjoyed by Italians in the northern-California metropolis was, however, unusual for the Italian element in American cities during this period.

For their part, Italian women dominated the garment industry. During the 1920s Italian women became the largest single group in the needle trades, having displaced the Jews. By 1937, according to David Dubinsky, president of the International Ladies' Garment Workers Union, immigrant and second-generation Italians numbered about 100,000 out of a total membership of 250,000 in the New York area.

Political patronage continued to provide economic benefits for Italian-colony residents in all large American cities. Organized crime was an even more lucrative source of income. On January 16, 1920, the Eighteenth Amendment and the Prohibition Enforcement Act (or Volstead Act) went into effect, forbidding the manufacture, sale, or transportation of intoxicating liquors. Supporters of the Eighteenth Amendment predicted that it would usher in a new era of "clean thinking and clean living." The results of Prohibition were far different from the lofty objectives envisioned by reformers. For young, upwardly mobile Italians and other urban ethnics, the "Noble Experiment" was a godsend, an opportunity to amass amounts of money and power undreamed of in earlier days. The Capones, O'Banions, and Lanskys were willing to take the risks necessary to build their businesses into successful concerns. Unlike many of their native-American contemporaries, the "businesses" they went into involved the illegal manufacture, importation, transportation, and sale of alcoholic beverages.

Identification of Italians with crime was not a new phenomenon. From the early years of immigration to the United States, Italians found themselves plagued by the fact that the American public identified them with Mafia activities and therefore with criminality.

In Southern Italy secret criminal societies like the Mafia formed part of the fabric of life. Like other newcomers to the United States, immigrant criminals attempted to re-create in their new homeland the institutions and the traditions with which they were familiar. Efforts to transport the Mafia to the Italian districts of American cities met with only limited success, for in the process of transferring across the ocean, familiar institutions underwent change. No matter how earnestly they tried, honest, hard-working peasants as well as criminal parasites found it impossible to re-create the Old World way of life in America's "Little Italys." The constant and heavy turnover of residents—as newcomers from overseas arrived to replace those who had moved out of the ethnic colony—prevented the formation of stable and unchanging colony life. Whereas change and mobility characterized American cities, the Sicilian Mafia and similar criminal societies thrived in a static environment like that in western Sicily. Furthermore, successful Mafia leaders generally did not find it necessary or desirable to move to the United States, except for short visits, until the 1920s, when Mussolini's Fascist regime forced many to relocate. In that decade and the one following, a number of Mafia chieftains migrated to the United States.

Homeland Mafia members who came to this country were attracted by a society that seemed to offer few barriers to economic success. They could have emigrated to a number of countries, but chose the United States instead of France, England, Brazil, or Argentina simply because they expected to get rich faster in America.

In the pre-Volstead years, American public awareness of Italian immigrant criminality concentrated on the activities of Black Hand extortion gangs and tales of "Mafia" blood oaths. More important in the long run than the more highly publicized Black Handers were the American-generation criminals whose growth to maturity coincided with the onset of Prohibition. These men, whether born in Italy or the New World, grew up as products of the American urban environment. They viewed themselves as Americans and chose to use crime as the vehicle to material success. They despised immigrant-colony criminals and had little desire to associate with or emulate the "greaseballs." Indeed, they did not hesitate to eliminate the old-timers whenever it was expedient to do so.

While public attention was directed elsewhere—to Black Hand bomb throwers and the like—these young men made their debuts into crime in the larger American environment involving gambling, prostitution, narcotics, and the labor wars. The experience they gained from such activities and the contacts they formed with members of other ethnic groups (as well as politicians and the police) in the years before 1920 served them well during the 1920s and 1930s. The vital ingredient came with the enactment of Prohibition. The "noble experiment" gave these young men the opportunity, which they exploited to the utmost, to eliminate the hated Italian-colony rivals and to establish powerful criminal syndicates, often in combination with Jewish associates.

Prohibition provided the means by which young ethnics entered the mainstream of American entrepreneurial crime, but repeal of the Eighteenth Amendment did not bring about a decline in their fortunes. After repeal—and, in fact, during the Prohibition era—criminal entrepreneurs engaged in other types of illegal but highly lucrative activities, including gambling, narcotics, prostitution, and business and labor racketeering. In the process of developing their businesses, syndicate leaders created organizations loosely and imperfectly patterned on those in existence in the legitimate business world. These organizations effectively filled the needs for which they were created.

Entrepreneurial crime offered an important avenue of upward economic mobility for members of the American generation. Although group unity and cooperative effort figured prominently in Italian successes within the highly competitive world of American syndicate crime during the 1920s and 1930s, certain individuals played roles of key importance. These men had a profound impact on the high level of criminal achievement Italians enjoyed during that era. The situation in entrepreneurial crime from the enactment of the Eighteenth Amendment until American entry into World War II exhibited considerable fluidity; during this period syndicate leaders were highly receptive to ideas that promised to maximize profits and reduce risks and uncertainty. Able businessmen of crime like Frank Costello, Charles "Lucky" Luciano, Frank Lazia, Al Capone, Joe Adonis, and John Torrio were innovators and experimenters. The institutions and procedures they and their associates created in cities throughout the country during the late twenties and the thirties provided the framework within which criminal syndicates have functioned ever since.

During the interwar decades Italians also had a significant impact in motion pictures, popular music, sports, and other fields of entertainment. The most famous romantic star of the silent-film era was Italian-born Rudolph Valentino. His dark good looks and torrid love scenes in his most memorable motion picture, *The Sheik* (1922), revolutionized the film industry and had an impact on American culture. When Valentino dragged Agnes Ayres by her hair into his tent to satisfy his Latin lust audiences went wild. It was unlike any love scene ever presented on film. Young men all around the country tried to imitate Valentino in appearance and romantic technique. Valentino's fame and influence far outlasted him. In 1926, at the height of his popularity and success, he was seized with an attack of gallstones while on a personal-appearance tour in New York City. Following an emergency operation he died of peritonitis at the age of thirty-one. Hollywood searched vainly for years for "another Valentino." Although one was never found another handsome and talented Italian American, Russ Colombo, in the early 1930s appeared well on his way to stardom both as an actor in film and as a popular singer. Once again a promising career tragically was cut short when Colombo suffered a fatal accident while on a hunting trip. In the late thirties Frank Sinatra, an even more talented singer and actor, began his long and successful career.

Although Italian Americans had been prominent in boxing for decades it was during the twenties and thirties that they moved into the front ranks in various other sports. Even in golf they produced several stars including Henry Ciuci; Johnny Revolta; Joe Turnesa; Tony Manero, who in 1936 won the American open championship with the lowest score ever made up to that time in a British or American open championship; and Gene Sarazen. During his long and outstanding career Sarazen won two American open championships, his first in 1922, three professional championships, and the British open championship. In 1932 he won both the American and the British open championships. In his June 17, 1982 column New York *Times* sportswriter Dave Anderson recalled Sarazen's many achievements, especially the double eagle. "Sarazen's double eagle two occurred at Augusta National's 15th hole during the final round of the 1935 Master's, which he went on to win in an 18-hole playoff with Craig Wood the next day. That double eagle," Anderson concluded in awe, "has endured as the single most spectacular shot in golf history."

In football Knute Rockne's great Notre Dame teams of 1928, 1929, and 1930 were directed by quarterback Frank Carideo and powered by fullback "Jumping Joe" Savoldi, who later became a premier professional wrestler. Carideo was an All-America selection in both 1929 and 1930, the second Italian American to gain this honor. The first was Mike Getto, a tackle for the University of Pittsburgh, who was chosen in 1928. In the 1930s Italian-American names dotted the lists of All-America selections. They included end John Orsi of Colgate in 1931; running back Angel Brovelli, St. Mary's, 1932; tackle Charles Ceppi, Princeton, 1933; guard Paul Tangora, Northwestern, 1935; fullback Nello Falaschi, Santa Clara, 1936; tackles Ed Franco of Fordham and Tony Matisi of Pittsburgh, 1937; end Bill Daddio of Pittsburgh and halfback Vic Bottari of California, 1938.

Among the numerous Italian Americans who starred in football for Fordham University during the 1930s was Vince Lombardi, a tough and durable guard and a key member of three of the Rams' finest teams. Lombardi later became one of professional football's best and most successful head coaches with the Green Bay Packers during the late fifties and sixties. Just as the Packers dominated the National Football League (NFL) during the Lombardi era, in the 1930s and 1940s the Chicago Bears were the class of the league. One of the pivotal games in football history was the Bears 73–0 rout of the Washington Redskins on December 8, 1940, for the NFL championship. The contest proved the superiority of the "T" over the single-wing and other formations. Among the players for the Bears were four Italian Americans: George Musso of tiny Millikin College in Illinois, a huge (280 pounds), very mobile guard and a star with the Bears for eleven years; another guard, Aldo Forte, of Montana; fullback Gary Famiglietti of Boston University; and Joe Maniaci, a fullback and place kicker from Fordham.

In the late thirties (1936–39) another Italian American, Stanford University's Hank Luisetti, revolutionized the game of basketball. "A great ball handler, he may have been the first to popularize the behind-the-back dribble. However, he is known for making famous an even more startling innovation, the one-handed shot."[10] Before Luisetti the one-handed shot generally was used only for layups. All other shots were taken with two hands. Luisetti proved it was possible to shoot as accurately with one hand as two and he could get the shot off more quickly. In addition, Luisetti could hit from almost anywhere, "not just set shots but running one-handers. He had the moves and body control to shoot while in the air, pioneering the jump shot, and he even had a jump hook shot in his repertoire."[11]

The San Francisco Italian community not only produced Luisetti but it also was the birthplace of three of the new York Yankees' most outstanding baseball players. They were second-baseman Tony Lazzeri, shortstop Frank Crosetti, and the incomparable Joe Di Maggio. Lazzeri was the first to join the Yankees. A powerful hitter as well as a fine infielder he was a member, along with Babe Ruth and Lou Gehrig, of the Yankees' famous "Murderers' Row" of the late twenties. Crosetti joined the team in the early thirties and with Lazzari provided the Yankees with an excellent double-play combination.

Di Maggio was a magnificent all-around ballplayer who could hit for average as well as with power, was a threat on the bases, and was perhaps the greatest defensive centerfielder in the history of professional baseball in America. In 1941 the "Yankee Clipper" set an amazing record when he hit safely in 56 consecutive games. Between May 15 and July 16 he collected 91 hits, including 15 home runs, in 223 times at bat for a .408 batting average. Of all of Di Maggio's many records and accomplishments this was without question the most outstanding. It is the one hitting record that most experts believe will never be matched or beaten. It was not simply what he did that made Di Maggio the greatest sports hero of his era but how he did it. On the ball field he made everything, even the seemingly impossible catch, look easy and effortless. Off the field he was quiet, modest, unassuming, and thoroughly honest. It was appropriate that when sportswriter Maury Allen published his best-selling *Where Have You Gone, Joe Di Maggio?* in 1975 he subtitled his admiring portrait of Di Maggio, the athlete and the man, "The Story of America's Last Hero."

During the twenties and thirties Italians realized few political successes comparable to their spectacular gains in syndicate crime or their achievements in various entertainment fields. The most successful Italian-American politician of his era was Fiorello La Guardia, elected in 1919 to the presidency of the Board of Aldermen of New York City. At that time, La Guardia's was the most important elective position that any Italian had gained in a major American city. Two years later La Guardia made an unsuccessful bid for mayor but the following year he won the seat he had earlier held in Congress. He served in the House of Representatives from 1923 to 1933, when he returned to New York and ran successfully for the office of mayor. For the next twelve years he provided the city with honest, efficient, and dynamic leadership. On his death in 1947 the New York *Times* reflected upon the impact of La Guardia's three terms as mayor:

The time was fourteen years ago. New York City was close to bankruptcy. In the city government itself there was an atmosphere of moral bankruptcy. The Seabury investigation, just ended, had disclosed the corruption and "easy graft" of sixteen years of Tammany rule. The city showed neglect. Ancient elevated lines were standing; there were no low-rent housing projects; only one public health center. This was the situation that the new reform Mayor, Fiorello Henry La Guardia, found when he walked into City Hall on January 1, 1934.

The time was one year and nine months ago [when La Guardia left office]. New York City was financially stable; its credit was good. The atmosphere in the city government had changed completely. The emphasis was on honest public service; commissioners worked instead of spending their time at race tracks or ball parks. The face of the city was altered. Most of the "Els" were down; there were new subways, bridges, parkways, fourteen low-rent housing projects, a modern public health service.[12]

La Guardia served New York with great distinction but he was not the first Italian American to become mayor of a major American city. In 1931, three years before La Guardia entered office in New York, Angelo Rossi became mayor of San Francisco. The son of Genoese immigrants, Rossi was born in the California mining town of Volcano, in Amador County, in 1878. Rossi's father died when the boy was six years old. Six years later, in 1890, young Angelo, his mother, and six brothers and sisters moved to San Francisco when the family-owned store burned to the ground. Angelo took a job as messenger boy for one of San Francisco's leading florists. By 1902 he had accumulated enough money to buy an interest in the company. Eventually he became sole proprietor and renamed the concern the Angelo Rossi Floral Company, which he operated until his death.

Rossi began his career in public service in 1914 when he was appointed to the San Francisco Playground Commission. He held a variety of appointive and elective offices in the following years. He became a member of the city's Board of Supervisors in 1921 and was re-elected in 1925 and 1929, when he became chairman of the Finance Committee.

On January 1, 1931, the Board of Supervisors elected Rossi to fill the unexpired term of incumbent mayor James Rolph, who resigned to become governor of California. Later in the year Rossi won election on his own and began the first of three capable and competent, if not brilliant, terms as mayor. "The greatest problem Rossi faced as mayor," Melvin Holli has noted, was unemployment. "Like other mayors of the day, he could do very little to help the situation despite his own personal feelings. His humanitarian concerns for the poor, sick, aged, and unemployed were well known in the city."[13] San Franciscans rewarded Rossi with a thirteen-year tenure in office, the second longest of any mayor in the city's history. Only Rolph, who occupied the office for nineteen years, served longer.

In 1936 yet another Italian American, Robert Maestri, became mayor of an important American port city, New Orleans. Maestri was born in New Orleans in 1889 of an Italian father and a French mother. Unlike La Guardia and Rossi, he entered politics only after a successful career in business. By the 1920s he was reputed to be one of the wealthiest men in New Orleans and perhaps the biggest property owner in the city. In the late twenties Maestri gravitated toward state politics and soon became an important member of the Huey Long political machine. According to political scientist V. O. Key, Maestri "provided money at critical times early in Long's career, became a power in Long's organization, and, after Long's death, mayor of New Orleans."[14]

Following Long's election as governor in 1928 Maestri was appointed chairman of the state's Conservation Committee, a position rich with patronage opportunities. In 1932 Long went on to serve in the United States Senate while Maestri remained on the Conservation Commission. Following "the Kingfish's" assassination in 1936 the machine turned out of office the anti-Long mayor of New Orleans, T. Semmes Walmsley, and replaced him with Maestri. During his time in office, Maestri was in his own words, "no reformer" but his tax policies and his success in cutting the city's bonded debt held a powerful appeal for businessmen, the middle class, and small homeowners. He was a hardworking, no-nonsense administrator who relished responsibility and liked to exercise authority. That Maestri "had learned his politics at the side of Huey Long" was, as historian Edward Haas has observed, quite evident. Maestri's administration "was a heterogéneous mixture of good government, unorthodox administration, spoils politics and concern for the people."[15]

Maestri served as mayor of New Orleans from 1936 to 1946. Thus for an eight-year period, from 1936 to 1943, Italian Americans guided the affairs of three of the largest and most important cities in the United States. The achievements of La Guardia, Rossi, and Maestri reflected the growing success enjoyed by Italian politicians during the depression years of the 1930s and the war years of the early 1940s. They also reflected a shift in party alignment that was taking place during this era. Rossi and Maestri were Democrats while La Guardia was a nominal Republican who was generally at odds with the party.

Although Italians had early ties with the Republican as well as the Democratic party this changed in the late twenties and thirties. The shift began in 1928 with the nomination of Al Smith as the Democratic party nominee for President. A Catholic, an opponent of Prohibition, and a Tammany Hall loyalist, the former four-time governor of New York had a powerful appeal for Italians and other urban immigrants. Smith lost the election but he cut into Republican strength in the urban North. Samuel Lubell has demonstrated that "before Smith the Democrats were little more of an urban party than were the Republicans."[16] The depression that began in 1929 speeded the "Revolt of the City," and by 1932, with the nomination and election of Franklin D. Roosevelt, the trend of 1928 was a decided fact. The relief programs of Roosevelt's New Deal convinced the urban masses that the government cared about their welfare and helped pull Italians and members of other ethnic groups into the Democratic party.

Increasing numbers of Italians were attracted to politics. Unfortunately, a number of successful Italian politicians during the interwar years had connections with, or were identified with, criminal elements. Thus during the thirties New York District Attorney Thomas E. Dewey helped expose Tammany Hall strongman Albert Marinelli as the creature—or, as some suggested, the creation —of underworld boss Charlie "Lucky" Luciano and associates. According to Warren Moscow, who at the time was a New York *Times* reporter, Marinelli replaced incumbent Harry Perry as Tammany Second Assembly district leader, on the Lower East Side, in a simple and direct manner:

> Perry's public payroll post was Chief Clerk of the City Court. One day two of Luciano's men walked into Perry's office in the old Tweed Court House, 70 feet from City Hall, patted the guns in their pockets, and said:
> "Perry, Lucky has a message for you. You're through."
> Perry gulped and muttered an "okay."[17]

In 1934 Marinelli also became County Clerk for New York County (Manhattan) and emerged as a power in the affairs of Tammany Hall. In just three years Marinelli was forced to resign his position as County Clerk.

Most ethnic-community youth who pursued careers in law became professionally familiar with still other criminals. Those who desired political office found syndicate leaders to be useful friends or contacts. Gangster-controlled votes held the balance of power in many core-area wards, where a favorable nod could secure a profitable career for an aspiring politician just as readily as a frown could ruin him.

The decade of the thirties was, for Italian-American immigrants and their children, not only a period of severe economic hardship and of political realignment but also of deep concern over the homeland's aggressive foreign policy under Mussolini's Fascist regime. Italian Americans became increasingly disillusioned as Italy drew closer diplomatically to Nazi Germany and became involved in foreign military ventures, first in 1935 in Ethiopia in defiance of League of Nations sanctions, then, after the outbreak of civil war in Spain in 1936, when Mussolini and his Nazi ally Adolf Hitler poured men and material into the country in support of General Francisco Franco against the Loyalists and their Russian Communist benefactors.

As the world slid toward war, Italians and other Americans wondered if the United States could remain aloof. It could not. Despite lavish outlays of money and extensive propaganda efforts by the Fascist government, Italian Americans fully supported the American war effort against Italy, as well as against Japan and Germany, after the United States entered World War II in December 1941. Of more than 600,000 Italian aliens in the United States, the American government deemed it necessary to intern only 228. An initial concern about the loyalty of unnaturalized Italians in the United States and a reluctance to employ them in war industries was soon overcome, and by the fall of 1942 the stigma of "enemy alien" status was removed.

Italian Americans proved their loyalty on the battlefield. An estimated 550,000 served in the American armed forces during the conflict. At least twelve received the Congressional Medal of Honor and another ten the Navy Cross. Marine Sergeant John Basilone of Raritan, New Jersey, who held off an entire Japanese regiment in Guadalcanal for three days, was awarded the Medal of Honor. General Douglas MacArthur called him "a one-man army." The Navy named a destroyer in his honor. It was one of two destroyers named for Italian-American Marine Medal-of-Honor winners during the war. The other was named for Corporal Anthony Damato of Shenandoah, Pennsylvania. Among other Italian-American heroes of World War II were Captain Don Gentile and Major A. Martini. Gentile, who flew nearly two hundred missions and was credited with shooting down forty-two Nazi planes, was one of the war's great American air aces. Martini's achievement was almost unbelievable. During a fifteen-minute air battle over Paris he shot down twenty-two Nazi planes.

The Italian-American community certainly contributed its share of heroes to the nation's war effort. With such sacrifices on the battlefield Italian Americans were determined that following the end of the war they would be accepted as first-class citizens.

CHAPTER 10

The Emergence of the Ethnic Italian

Following the end of World War II soldiers, sailors, and other servicemen returned to civilian life and a grateful and appreciative society. There was strong bipartisan support for Congressional passage, in June 1944, of the Servicemen's Readjustment Act, the so-called G.I. Bill of Rights. "A grateful nation," Arthur Link has observed, "poured out its resources to help its former servicemen."[1]

The G.I. Bill was the vital element that made it possible for many Italian Americans and also members of other ethnic groups to enter the middle class. Thousands of Italian Americans made use of the G.I. Bill to attend college, most to become the first in their family to receive a degree. The degrees made it possible to qualify for careers in law, medicine, or large business corporations. Ex-servicemen also made use of low-interest loans from the Veterans' Administration (the VA) or from the Federal Housing Administration (the FHA) to leave core-area Little Italys and join other Americans of their generation in the suburbs. One Italian American recalled: "The G.I. Bill gave many of our men the economic ladder to go up and the FHA gave them the money to get out." FHA or VA financing "made it possible to live in a house that had three cubic inches of grass and assured status. If you moved to suburbia, you would finally find the recognition and acceptance from the larger America that the people in the old neighborhood had always wanted." Those who wanted to remain "in the old neighborhood," on the other hand, found that the only source of loan money was "through the building and loans that the ethnics themselves created and that necessitated a one third down payment."[2] This was because, at least until the mid-1960s, both the FHA and VA preferred to loan money for the construction of new housing in suburban areas, not for the purchase of existing structures in the urban core. The latter were considered to be bad risks, in large part because of the presence of what the FHA Operation Manual termed "inharmonious racial or national groups."[3] In other words, increasing numbers of blacks from the rural American South and Spanish-speaking newcomers from Mexico and Puerto Rico during and after World War II flocked into inner-city neighborhoods which, in the view of financial institutions and federal bueaucrats, made the entire core a bad risk for everything except public housing.

This fact is ironic because the ethnic consciousness that formed in the black ghettos of American cities during the 1950s and 1960s played a central role in the development of the ethnic awareness that emerged among Italians, Poles, and other white groups in the late sixties and seventies. As one group leader complained in the press in November 1971: "The revolution of the '60s has seen the blacks achieve some measure of acceptance in their struggle for equal treatment. . . . Is it too much for Italo-Americans to ask for their fair share of human dignity from that same community?"[4] This demand grew out of the conviction that group pride and the application of group pressure enabled blacks to gain benefits that other groups ought to share. Thus journalist Ken Auletta who was a New York City politician in the 1960s and 1970s recalls that "black power demands were followed by community and then ethnic group demands from poor Hispanics, Jews, and Italo Americans."[5]

This is not, of course, what earlier generations of Italian Americans believed was the most effective way to gain acceptance. Previously, many would have fully agreed with observations novelist John Fante made about his immigrant-generation father in a magazine article printed in the late 1930s:

I look up at him in amazement. Is this man my father? Why, look at him! Listen to him! He reads with an Italian inflection! He's wearing an Italian mustache. I have never realized it until this moment, but he looks exactly like a Wop. His suit hangs carelessly in wrinkles upon him. Why the deuce doesn't he buy a new one? And look at his tie! It's crooked. And his shoes; they need a shine. And for the Lord's sake, will you look at his pants! They're not even buttoned in front. And, oh damn, damn, damn, you can see those dirty old suspenders that he won't throw away. Say, mister, are you really my father? You there, why you're such a little guy, such a runt, such an old looking fellow! You look exactly like one of those immigrants carrying a blanket! You can't be *my* father.[6]

While the youngsters of Fante's generation typically were ashamed of their strange-looking parents and tried to hide their Italian origins, *their* children are different. In the homogenized environment of suburbia, Italian Americans of the third generation in search of their self-identity have re-examined the experiences of the immigrant generation and take pride in what their parents abhored: the peasant origins of their grandparents and the miserable living and working conditions they encountered and endured in core-area tenement neighborhoods.

Italian Americans have shared fully in the general prosperity the nation has enjoyed since World War II. Movement out of the ethnic districts slowed during the 1930s because of the Depression and during the 1940s because of wartime housing shortages, but by the 1950s the process had accelerated, and the formerly heavy concentrations of Italians in immigrant neighborhoods has thinned out. Thus although Chicago's Near West Side community continues in existence, its population is greatly reduced. The district held an Italian immigrant population of 12,995 in 1920; the same area contained a *combined* total of first- and second-generation Italians of 5,140 in 1960 and only 1,806 ten years later. In Boston's Italian district, the North End, the population decreased by 45.8 percent between 1950 and 1960, and by 40 percent in the next ten years. The decline, according to Spencer Di Scala, is attributable "to younger people and couples moving out of the area." The general tendency has been "for more established persons to move out and for newer arrivals from Italy to take their place."[7]

Di Scala's observations illustrate the altered function of the limited number of core-area ethnic districts still in existence. The typical community is largely a collection of the elderly whose ties to the area and advancing age discourages them from leaving; a residue of young adults, some single, some married with children, who remain to look after their parents; local businessmen; political patronage job holders; and a small number of recent immigrants for whom the neighborhood is a low-cost area of first settlement in the city. Most of the ambitious members of the younger generation have left the colony to live in other parts of the city and the suburbs.

In recent years a new trend has emerged in such communities as Boston's North End and Chicago's Near West Side. While upwardly mobile Italian Americans continue to move out of the colony in search of a better life, non-Italian young upper-middle-class suburbanites are moving in. They are flocking "into the North End (and the surrounding waterfront) because it has become very fashionable to live there. . . . Many of the old buildings are being purchased and renovated by developers." Di Scala finds this process "disturbing" because after the rehabilitation has been completed long-established Italian residents "can no longer afford to pay the high rents" and are forced to move out.[8]

For the adventurous ex-suburbanites the core area is a pleasant and relatively inexpensive environment in which to live and raise their children. Ironically, even some third-generation Italian Americans in search of their roots have been attracted back to the neighborhoods their grandparents and parents worked so hard to escape. In an article entitled "Young People Find a 'Good Deal,' West Side Community Gets Second Chance," the Chicago *Tribune* on August 22, 1976, proclaimed the reclamation of Chicago's Near West Side Italian neighborhood, which "just ten years ago was called a slum, an area which many had written off" as one that could never be saved. "Today the Near West Side is a viable, healthy community of 10,000 persons getting an economic shot in the arm at every turn from both public and private capital." With the movement of middle-class families into the area and the departure of low-income residents, more than twenty million dollars was poured into the community, "giving rise to shopping centers, apartment-condominium complexes, and restored and renovated apartment buildings." The new residents concluded that they had found the best of all possible worlds—"a social oasis, amid parks, schools, a hospital, and a score of ethnic shops."[9] In addition, their new residences are located near the city's central business district, the Loop, where many of them worked. By 1976 Chicago's Near West Side, like Boston's North End, was well on its way to becoming "chic." In this respect both locations were following a pattern similar to that in New Orleans. The French Quarter which some seventy-five years ago contained the Crescent City's most miserable Italian slum district, Little Palermo, has long since become a fashionable residential community as well as the city's major tourist attraction.

The return migration from the suburbs of middle- and upper-income whites, especially young married couples, has played an important role in the break-up of some working-class Italian neighborhoods. Other Italian communities have dispersed because of the influx of blacks, Hispanics, and southern whites. Italians and other new immigrant groups applied to these low-income newcomers many of the same attitudes that Anglo-Saxons and members of old immigrant groups had earlier exhibited toward them. Italians do not feel they are responsible for racism in America. In fact, they point out that during the immigrant era their parents or grandparents frequently were victims of racism. Prejudice against blacks has been tinged with envy and sometimes grudging respect for the effective use they have made of political pressure to gain economic and other benefits.

Recent demands by Italian Americans have significantly not

included a return to the days of free immigration. The acrimony connected with the passage of the National Origins Act of 1924, which set up restrictive quotas, was in large measure related to the attitude that Italians and other Southern and Eastern Europeans were somehow less-acceptable citizens than were arrivals from other countries. Rather than the system itself, what infuriated Italians was the pitifully small quota assigned Italians (3,845 per year). Complaints dwindled with the enactment of the 1965 immigration law, which gave all nations the same access to an overall yearly quota but assigned priority status to immediate relatives of American citizens and resident aliens as well as to professionals and skilled workers in short supply among the native population.

During the decades since the end of World War II more than 500,000 Italian immigrants have entered the United States. Nearly half (228,000) came in the decade following the passage of the 1965 law. The 1970 United States Census counted over four million first- and second-generation Italian Americans and found them in every state in the Union, although almost 70 percent still resided in the heavily industrialized and urban Northeast.

Italian immigrants and their offspring no longer necessarily lived in central-city districts, but they still tended to live in or around major cities. In 1970 nearly 2.3 million first- and second-generation Italian Americans resided in only twelve metropolitan areas; one million of them lived in the New York Metropolitan area, the rest in Boston, Providence, Buffalo, Rochester, Philadelphia, Pittsburgh, Cleveland, Detroit, Chicago, San Francisco–Oakland, and Los Angeles–Long Beach.

Among Italian Americans in the postwar decades traditional immigrant community institutions had, with the exception of the Catholic Church, fallen into disuse. Mutual-benefit societies and the Italian-language press, vibrant and influential institutions during the immigrant era, had by the 1960s come on hard times. A survey of more than three hundred Italian residents of Chicago's Near West Side found that none of the people interviewed belonged to an Italian fraternal organization and none read a foreign-language newspaper, nor did anyone else in their families. Many were not even aware of the existence of the two largest Italian fraternal groups: the Sons of Italy and the Italo-American National Union. A sizable minority claimed to own life-insurance policies, but with American companies. Only the Catholic Church continued to attract support: almost without exception residents claimed membership in one of the three Catholic churches in the area, although religious observance appeared to be more common among the older generation than among their children.

The elderly still obtained news of events in Italy from Italian-language radio broadcasts and from a monthly paper, *Fra Noi*, which regularly printed a summary page in Italian. *Fra Noi* is put out by a Catholic religious order, and during the mid-sixties was the only city publication written about and for Italian Americans. Later, the weekly *L'Italia* was started; by 1979 its circulation had reached 6000. The Italian-language press has been somewhat stronger in the East, where Italian immigrants continue to arrive and congregate. Yet only New York's *Il Progresso Italo-Americano*, which has a national as well as a local edition, publishes daily. *Il Progresso*'s circulation in 1979 was 58,251; the next largest Italian-language paper, the *Italian Echo* of Providence, Rhode Island, a weekly, had a circulation of only 23,000.

Italians remain loyal to the Catholic Church, although they do not exert a leadership within it in proportion to their numbers. In 1972 more than half of an estimated 21 million Italian Americans of all generations were still active Catholics (about 20 percent of the total Catholic population in the country), but there were only nine bishops of Italian background in the entire United States. In contrast, Irish Americans comprised 17 percent of the Catholic Church's membership and provided more than half of its bishops.

In 1970 Nathan Glazer noted a basic factor responsible for the underrepresentation of Italians among the leadership of the Church: the number of Italian priests remained small. While they drew high marks in several categories, including church attendance, support of parochial education, and acceptance of the Irish-dominated Church's cultural outlook, Italian Americans were found to lag "in one respect—they do not provide large numbers of priests." While this underrepresentation might change, "it seems likely that one reason for the small weight of Italians in the Catholic Church—aside from the influence of the superlative organizational and bureaucratic skills of the Irish—is the fact that so few of them enter the Church and are available for further advancement."[10]

Multi-ethnic parochial schools, parishes, and church-sponsored social organizations have encouraged marriage with non-Italian Catholics. Intermarriage among Italians in Buffalo, for example, increased from 12 percent in 1930 to 27 percent in 1950 to 50 percent in 1960. Intermarriage among third-generation Italian Americans in the United States, according to a survey conducted in 1963–64, was 58 percent. Even when they marry outside the group, however, Italians tend to remain within the Church and choose a mate of either Irish, German, or Polish background.

Third-generation Italian Americans are not only more likely than members of earlier generations to marry outside the ethnic group, they also are more readily disposed to dissolve unsuccessful marriages. Divorce is no longer an unthinkable and unacceptable option.

The contemporary Italian-American family tends to resemble the smaller, more egalitarian, child-centered units typical of the American middle class. Even among the working class the third generation is only "slightly more patriarchal than other lower class families but still strives toward the 'democratic family' ideal."[11]

In keeping with the native-American norm, the third-generation Italian-American husband "is likely to have a spouse who bears no resemblance to the old immigrant woman who considered herself entirely dedicated to her husband's wishes and caprices, and he accepts this behavior as proper." Marital roles generally "are divided along sex lines, but there are many areas—including child-rearing and discipline, cooking, cleaning—in which at times the two spouses exchange or complement roles." The family is "decidedly child-centered. The children are deliberately instructed in the ways of the American middle-class." Thus education is highly valued. "Indeed, in reaction to the lack of education in the family background, the parents are often obsessively concerned with the success of the children in school."[12] If they do not already live in the suburbs one of the family's goals is to move, generally to an industrial suburb located adjacent to the city. Nevertheless, contact still is maintained with parents, grandparents, and friends still living in the old neighborhood.

Suburbanite Italian Americans also still drive to core-area neighborhood stores on shopping expeditions for olive oil, salami, cheese, artichokes, pepperoni, and other "authentic" food unavailable in the shopping-center supermarket. They also return to "the old neighborhood" to participate in religious festivals and celebrations. In New York City the main social event of the year for the various Italian colonies is the six-day Festival of San Gennaro, celebrated each September along Mulberry Street, on Manhattan's Lower East Side. Each day and night the narrow, booth-lined street is choked with milling crowds of people. The principal pastime is the patronage of canopied booths bulging with pizza, sausage-and-eggplant sandwiches, zeppolo, lemon ices, tortoni, torrone, balloons, parasols, dolls, hats, chances on stuffed animals, chances on automobiles. Neighborhood vegetable stores, cheese shops, restaurants, and bars also enjoy a thriving business as do Ferris wheels temporarily erected on parking lots. While San Gennaro is a Neapolitan *festa* the descendants of Italians from other provinces and non-Italians are all welcome to participate in the festivities, to watch the fireworks displays, and to observe the procession and high mass on the sixth day which mark the culmination of the celebration.

Italians and others alike flock to the San Gennaro, San Rocco, Santa Rossilia, and other feast days from remote parts of New York City and its suburbs and even from neighboring states. Many are attracted by the wide variety and high quality of the food in stalls and local restaurants, little realizing or even caring that what they consume is not typical peasant fare. Food is also the main attraction at ethnic festivals held annually, if not more frequently, in various Eastern and Middle-Western cities. One such celebration, a "Festa Italiana," was held on Navy Pier in Chicago from August 21 to 23, 1981. A crowd estimated at 100,000 "came from all Chicago neighborhoods, from the suburbs, and beyond" to observe an idealized vision of life "in the old days" in core-area Italian neighborhoods. "The entire south end of Navy Pier was transformed into one gigantic Italian neighborhood of another era. . . . The food stands emitting aromas of Italian cooking assailed you at every step." The crowd had a choice of home-made pasta, baked clams, stuffed aritchokes, fried zucchini, fried calamari, and "Italian sausage with peppers, Italian ices, cannoli, cookies and other delicacies." The festival, according to the chairman of the sponsoring organization, celebrated "Italian-American life and provided a glimpse of our culture."[13]

The contemporary hunger for Italian-American culture does not extend to literature, nor does it generally include study of the Italian language. Only a rapidly dwindling minority is able to use, or willing to learn, Italian. Third-generation Italian Americans who take a fierce pride in the privations and obstacles their grandparents endured and overcame in adjusting to living and working conditions in urban America exhibit limited interest in the numerous novels that have been written over the past half-century. Italian-American writers, Mario Puzo has observed, "complain that they do not receive the encouragement from their ethnic group that Jewish writers receive from theirs." As a case in point Puzo described a humiliating experience one such novelist (perhaps himself) was forced to endure. The author produced a work which the *New York Times Book Review* hailed as "a small classic of Italians and their children in this country." Critics near and far sang the author's parises. Unfortunately,

the book was not a popular success and did not even get a paperback sale. However, the Anglo-Saxon editor of a reprint house owned by an

American-Italian wanted very much to buy it. He cunningly decided to bring publisher and writer together (two lovable *paisanos* after all) at a small party. The publisher surely would want a wider public for a fellow American-Italian who had so immortalized his countrymen in a work of art. The writer, a suspicious Southern Italian-American, would surely be flattered and would lower his asking price enough to make publishing such a noncommercial novel feasible. (Any novel labeled a small classic is automatically classified noncommercial.)

And so the publisher, a dapper little man dressed in those conservative grays and blacks which most middle-class American-Italians touchingly believe erase all traces of greenhornishness, was confronted by the gloweringly suspicious writer. To the astonishment of the Anglo-Saxon editor, the two lovable *paisanos* immediately treated each other with unmistakable rudeness. The publisher, a padrone, after all, was condescendingly not interested in backing a "loser." The writer, with peasant Sicilian insolence, asked the publisher if his father's shovel was still around the house and if so did he use it to dig up the dung his firm was putting out. The "small classic" remains out of reach of the general public to this day.[14]

Puzo's beautifully written and insightful *The Fortunate Pilgrim* is one of the finest novels written about Italian-colony life. Yet its publication went largely unnoticed by the reading public. Although it was finally reprinted in paperback, after the spectacular success of the novel and two-part motion picture, *The Godfather*, *The Fortunate Pilgrim* remains little more than a "small classic."

Of the numerous talented Italian-American writers who, since the 1930s, have attempted to describe and understand immigrant family and neighborhood life only Pietro Di Donato enjoyed popular success—and that only for his first novel, *Christ in Concrete*. Published in 1939, the book became a best seller and later a motion picture.

Apparently Italian Americans prefer the idealized reminiscences provided by civic and religious celebrations to the stark and often painfully realistic descriptions of immigrant existence offered by novels such as *The Fortunate Pilgrim*. The success of *The Godfather* underlines this fact. A formula book, indifferently written but amply spiced with sex and violence and laced with a mixture of

myth and reality, it fitted the public conception of Italian criminality. The novel and the subsequent films held a powerful appeal
for the American public, third-generation Italian Americans included, and yielded the fame and fortune Puzo intended the project
to produce.

What members of the third generation, most of whom "have
never known anything but middle-class life, . . . seek is the prestige
that was denied their parents."[15] Thus Italian Americans now
concentrate on campaigns to eliminate real or imagined social
prejudice and ethnic slurs against them as well as on opening up
areas of economic, political, or cultural activity hitherto closed to
them. In the American system benefits accrue through application
of group pressure. During the era of the big-city machines, patronage jobs and other short-term benefits were the rewards of political
power. Now that the Italian-American group identifies with the
middle class, promises of pick-and-shovel jobs and neighborhood
conveniences like bathhouses and small parks have long since lost
their attraction.

Perhaps because Italian Americans no longer are objects of the
unyielding hostility and fierce prejudice that were encountered by
new immigrants at the turn of the century, they feel free to pro-
claim their ethnicity and to search for their roots. One result has
been the formation, in various urban centers, of organizations that
in the late 1960s and early 1970s directed rallies and demonstra-
tions to protest the Italian-American image being projected in the
media, especially television, movies, and newspapers.

Many Italian Americans, particularly in the East, firmly believe
that group members are passed over in favor of blacks and Hispanics, who, they feel, are admitted to prestigious academic institutions or are given jobs for which Italian Americans are better
qualified. Thus a study conducted in the mid-1970s found that in
New York City, where Italian Americans composed 21 percent of
the population, "less than five percent of the City University system had Italian-American administrators, while 34 percent of the
student body is Italian-American." It is a bitter pill to swallow that

"other American minorities have been protected by various Government agencies from just such job discrimination, but it seems, the Italian-American plight has been largely ignored."[16]

When viewed from the perspective of the black experience in the South or the Chicano in the Southwest the discrimination white ethnics faced in the 1970s recedes in scale and importance. This, however, is not the significant point. White ethnics feel that for decades they played by the rules of society (as formulated by the dominant WASP element) and just when they were on the verge of "making it" economically and socially society changed the rules. According to the new rules, ethnic background (that is, color) took on at least as much importance as hard work and other virtues formerly extolled in school. Whether or not that was an accurate assessment of the intent and the results of civil-rights legislation enacted in the 1960s, "the rude awakening," Columbia University Professor Fred Barbaro noted in 1974, led at least some "in this subgroup to seek affiliation with Italian-American organizations although they may share little but a common ancestry."[17]

Contrary to popular belief Italian Americans, and members of other white ethnic groups, have achieved significant economic success. The general prosperity that the nation enjoyed in the postwar period and into the 1970s benefited Italians as well as other Americans. Many veterans of World War II, the Korean conflict, and Vietnam used the G.I. Bill to finance college educations and take professional training; they obtained jobs in industry or started businesses of their own. A 1963–64 study of occupational patterns among Italian Americans found that 48 percent of the respondents were employed in white-collar jobs and 52 percent in blue-collar jobs. In contrast, 26 percent of the fathers of the respondents held white-collar positions, 71 percent were in blue-collar jobs, and 3 percent were employed as farmers. Furthermore, Italians in working-class occupations had shifted from unskilled to semiskilled and skilled jobs.

Based on research conducted by the National Opinion Research

Center (NORC), of which he was Director, Andrew Greeley in 1974 stated that "Italians have reached the national average in the percentage of those who have become managers or owners or professional or technical workers." Referring to studies conducted by NORC over the previous several years, Greeley concluded that the evidence "leaves little doubt" that Italians "have moved rapidly into the upper-middle class of American society during the last two decades."[18]

In 1975 Greeley presented the findings of a survey NORC conducted for the Ford Foundation in the correlation between religion, ethnic background, and income. According to the NORC figures, Italian Catholic families ranked third from the top. With an average family income of $11,748, Italians followed Jews ($13,340) and Irish Catholics ($12,426). Baptists ranked lowest ($8,693) of the seventeen groups surveyed. (See Table 11.)

In their move up the economic ladder Italians have followed, on a smaller scale and a generation later, a pattern noted among Jews, whereby "the children of storekeepers and small businessmen went to college and became professionals." Italians are attending college in ever-increasing numbers. By the 1970s they comprised approximately one-third of the students in the City University of New York system and half of the student body at Fordham University. As a result of their stronger qualifications and better educational background, the grandchildren of Italian immigrants "are moving into the professions and the higher white collar fields."[19] They are filling the great bureaucracies of government and business.

Italian Americans are also prominent in such glamour fields as advertising, sports, and entertainment. Four of the most successful motion-picture directors in recent years have been the Italian Americans Francis Ford Coppola (*Godfather I* and *II* and *Apocalypse Now*), Martin Scorsese (*Taxi Driver* and *Raging Bull*), Brian De Palma (*Carrie*), and Michael Cimino (*The Deer Hunter*). They have not, one writer has noted, "made the kind of glossy features Hollywood usually bankrolls." Rather than technical tours de force like *Star Wars* and *Jaws* their films "emphasize the elemental

Table 11. Religion, Ethnic Background, and Income

Religious/Ethnic Group	Average Family Income (1974 dollars)
Jews	$13,340
Irish Catholics	12,426
Italian Catholics	11,748
German Catholics	11,632
Polish Catholics	11,298
Episcopalians	11,032
Presbyterians	10,976
Slavic Catholics	10,826
British Protestants	10,354
French Catholics	10,188
Methodists	10,103
German Protestants	9,758
Lutherans	9,702
Scandinavian Protestants	9,597
Irish Protestants	9,147
Baptists	8,693

Chicago *Tribune*, October 19, 1975.

themes and values that imbue our culture with continuity and traditions that burst with importance and meaning."[20] This characterization stands in sharp contrast to an earlier Italian-American director, Frank Capra, whose incurable optimism led some critics to brand his films "Capra-corn." Yet in a career that bridged the decades from the 1920s to the 1950s, the Sicilian-born Capra was responsible for some of the finest films Hollywood ever produced. They include *Arsenic and Old Lace, Lost Horizon, Mr. Smith Goes to Washington, It's a Wonderful Life,* and three that won Capra Oscars for Best Director: *Mr. Deeds Goes to Town, You Can't Take It With You,* and *It Happened One Night.* The latter was one of the most stunning successes in film history. Columbia regarded it as a throwaway, a second feature on double bills. No one at the studio except Capra had faith in the film. It won four major Academy Awards. In addition to Capra's award for Best Director these awards went to Clark Gable, for Best Actor, Claudette Colbert for Best Actress, to the producer for the Best Film of 1934.

None of Capra's movies, however, was about Italians. Capra did not make gangster movies and the limited number of films produced about Italians in the 1930s and 1940s generally were about organized crime. Yet Italian actors usually were not hired to portray Italian mobsters. Thus the male lead in the two most famous and influential gangsters movies of the era were Jews—Edward G. Robinson in *Little Caesar* (1930) and Paul Muni in *Scarface* (1932). This tendency has changed dramatically in the last decade. Italian Americans are now, as one writer has phrased it, "Hollywood's Favorite Ethnic Group." The group stereotype has shifted from gangster to "soulful underdog" and a steady stream of movies has appeared with Italian-American heroes, who often have been portrayed by Italian-American actors, another significant change from the thirties.[21] The most successful of these films probably have been *Saturday Night Fever*, starring John Travolta; *Rocky I, II* and *III*, with Sylvester Stallone; and *The Godfather I* and *II* with Al Pacino and Robert De Niro. Other actors of Italian-American heritage include Paul Sorvino, Tony Lo Bianco, Anne Bancroft, Liza Minnelli, Talia Shire, Ben Gazzara, Richard Conte, and two who have combined singing and acting careers, Dean Martin and Frank Sinatra.

Sinatra has been an enormously talented performer, both as a singer and an actor, but this fact, as Peter Marris suggests, may be only one of the reasons Italian Americans hold him in high esteem. "The people of the West End [of Boston], for instance, admired Frank Sinatra, because they felt he still defied conventional society and remained faithful to the more or less disreputable friends who had given him his start: he had forced the [outside] world to accept him without compromise."[22]

Since at least the early 1940s Sinatra has, according to his "unauthorized biographer" Earl Wilson, "had the world on a string, and he did it all—or nearly all—by himself."[23] By 1981 Freddie Brisson would in all seriousness claim that his pal Frank Sinatra "is more powerful than the president or the pope. His power is unseen, but it is greater."[24]

A man of fierce loyalty to family and friends "the King" has always insisted on living by his own rules. Part of his mystique among Italians and non-Italians alike has been Sinatra's widely publicized reputation for being the "intimate of Presidents and Mafia dons."[25] Sinatra has explained his reported association with such underworld figures as Lucky Luciano and Sam Giancana by stating: "I was brought up to shake a man's hand when I am introduced to him without investigating his past."[26] According to syndicate crime expert and former New York Police Department member Ralph Salerno the situation is not this simple or innocent, as least as far as the syndicate members are concerned. "A really big celebrity, like Frank Sinatra, is of tremendous public relations value" to the underworld. When Sinatra is seen with a reputed syndicate man, Salerno notes, "no one can think there is any other connection between them but genuine friendship. And when he is also welcome in Washington, few can really believe that his other friends are as bad as their reputations."[27]

During the decades since World War II, Italian-American crime-syndicate groups have continued to tap traditional sources of illegal enterprise such as gambling, loan-sharking, narcotics, bootlegging (of cigarets, furs, and other items along with the prohibition-era staple, alcohol), and racketeering. Italians have also moved into lucrative new areas of criminal activity, such as the theft and sale of securities. Criminal syndicates have also, in recent decades, devoted increasing attention to legitimate business. Whether this represents an effort to "launder" money obtained from illegal activities, as a means to infiltrate and corrupt legitimate enterprises, or as an effort to leave a sordid life and gain respectability is a matter of dispute among experts on syndicate crime.

It is evident that changes are taking place within the world of syndicate crime. The generation of leaders who grew to maturity during the prohibition era and who helped create the "Combination" during the thirties, clung tenaciously to power into the post–World War II decades. Those who were not killed in the periodic power struggles are, like Carlo Gambino (who died of a heart attack at the age of seventy-six in 1976), succumbing to the ravages of old age. Whether a younger generation of able entrepreneurs will emerge to dispute the challenge of blacks and Hispanics, especially in the highly lucrative narcotics traffic, is not clear. Efforts by younger leaders to inject new ideas and techniques into syndicate operations suffered a setback on June 28, 1971, when Joe Colombo, who took the offensive and led Italian-American protesters against the FBI and others who—he claimed—slurred the Italian-American name, was shot three times and paralyzed by a black gunman at an Italian-American Unity Day parade in New York.

The jobs created and money accumulated as well as the political contacts made and used by rum-runners and other syndicate members contributed significantly to the economic and political gains realized by the Italian-American community in the 1920s and 1930s. By the postwar era the community no longer needed such activities for its economic well-being. By the sixties and seventies Italian Americans did not suffer the job discrimination earlier generations had to overcome. Although bias still exists, especially in the East, able and ambitious youngsters are qualifying for and obtaining positions as corporation executives, army officers, lawyers, CPAs, university professors, and physicians. This was not, however, the situation in Frank Costello's day.

Costello, who was born Francesco Castiglia in Calabria in 1891, emigrated to the United States with his parents when he was four years old and grew to maturity in Manhattan's East Harlem Italian district. Early in his life he turned to crime and by World War I Costello's gambling operations were firmly established and he was beginning to form his unparalleled network of political contacts.

During the twenties and thirties Costello, along with a small group of other ambitious and able young Italians, Jews, Irish, and members of other ethnic groups, helped revolutionize American crime. By the late 1940s Costello's illicit business operations netted millions of dollars but, "in constant trouble with the federal government over taxes, and subject to the ministrations of an analyst," he was "most concerned with achieving respectability."[28] This driving "personal ambition," as Gay Talese labeled Costello's quest for respectability, would always elude the so-called "Prime Minister of the Underworld."[29]

Although Italian Americans remain a major, even a dominant, force in syndicate crime, the glory years of Costello, Capone, Luciano, Torrio, and other innovative and highly capable leaders have long since receded into the past. The syndicates also do not exert the power and influence in urban politics, at least in New York City, that they did in earlier generations. Longtime political analyst Warren Moscow, a New York *Times* reporter from 1930 through 1952, noted that "every Tammany Hall leader, from Mike Kennedy in 1942 to and including Carmine G. De Sapio in 1949, was selected by or with the aid and approval of Costello." Unfortunately for the syndicate and for the Tammany Hall organization itself, De Sapio tried to "run a good, clean show" and instituted sweeping reforms within the Democratic Party which had the effect of shifting control from the regular organization to the party membership itself. Thus, "by the election of 1965, the underworld control of, or alliance with the political machinery, born in the days of bootlegging, had virtually disappeared."[30]

Even De Sapio himself eventually fell victim to the reforms he instituted and was stripped of his position as leader of Tammany and, finally, even his district leadership. Nevertheless, Italians have enjoyed considerable success in politics since World War II. As Fiorello La Guardia's success represented the coming of age of Italian Americans in city politics before World War II, John O. Pastore's success has represented their acceptance on state and national levels in the decades since the War. In 1946 Pastore

became the first Italian American elected governor of a state;
Charles Poletti and Louis W. Capelli had preceded him as elected
lieutenant governors. Pastore, whose parents emigrated from
Southern Italy to Providence, Rhode Island, in 1899, eight years
before John was born, was chosen as a running mate for incumbent
governor, J. Howard McGrath, and within a year had succeeded
McGrath, who resigned to become United States Solicitor General.
In 1946 and again in 1948 Pastore was reelected governor, and in
1950 he was ready to seek national office. Although Italian Americans had served in the House of Representatives at least as early as
1887, when New York's Francis B. Spinola began the first of his
three terms, Pastore was the first elected Italian-American Senator.
He served with distinction from 1950 until his retirement in 1976.
Pastore's victories, like those of La Guardia, were based on an
ability to appeal to Italians and non-Italians alike. Samuel Lubell
noted as early as 1949 that from the beginning of his career in
state government "Pastore set about building 'a record, not an
organization.' By doing so, he made himself the pride not only of
the Italo-Americans alone but of all Rhode Island."[31] As a result
of the achievements of La Guardia and Pastore no city, state, or
national office is beyond the reach of Italian politicians.

Thus in politics as in most areas of activity Italian Americans
have, by the 1980s, met and overcome serious obstacles and
achieved a hard-earned place in society. All members of the group
have not, of course, enjoyed economic success but as a group
Italian Americans have entered the mainstream of American life.
The recent emphasis on Italian-American ethnicity is a part of this
adjustment. It appears that most Americans now want to be considered ethnics. Ethnicity, Andrew Greeley observed in 1975, "has
become almost fashionable."[32] Even WASPs claim ethnicity.
Thus the most comprehensive study of the subject, *The Harvard
Encyclopedia of American Ethnic Groups*, in 1981 examined the
experience of more than one hundred ethnic groups that live in the
United States. Among the groups, along with blacks, Puerto
Ricans, Italians, and Poles, are Appalachians, Southerners, and

Yankees. These last are the hated and envied WASPs (White Anglo-Saxon Protestants). To Italians, blacks, and Poles, WASPs are not ethnics. WASPs are the establishment and to them ethnicity is nonestablishment. Pulitzer-prize-winning columnist Ellen Goodman recognizes this aspect of the "new ethnicity," as she calls it, when she judges it to be part of "a long-term love-hate relationship with the dominant WASP culture." On the one hand Italians and other white ethnics would like to possess what they perceive WASPs to have: "power, money, control and the ability never to be gauche even when we are rude. But, on the other hand, we hold the unalterable opinion that it isn't worth it if the price is eating cucumber sandwiches at weddings."[33]

Notes

Preface

1. Eric F. Goldman, *Rendezvous with Destiny: A History of Modern American Reform* (New York, 1952), p. 30.

2. Alfred Aversa, Jr., "Italian Neo-Ethnicity: The Search for Self-Identity," *Journal of Ethnic Studies*, VI (Summer 1978), 49.

Chapter 1: Early Italians in America

1. Samuel Eliot Morison, *Admiral of the Ocean Sea: A Life of Christopher Columbus* 2 vols., (Boston, 1942), I, p. 308.

2. Quoted in Samuel Eliot Morison, *The Oxford History of the American People* (New York, 1965), p. 31.

3. Quoted in Edmundo O'Gorman, *The Invention of America: An Inquiry into the Historical Nature of the New World and the Meaning of Its History* (Bloomington, Ind., 1961), p. 166, n. 98.

4. Amerigo Vespucci, *The Letters of Amerigo Vespucci and Other Documents Illustrative of His Career*, Clement R. Markham, trans. and ed. (London, 1894), p. XXXIX.

5. Morison, *Admiral of the Ocean Sea*, II, p. 417.

6. Denis Mack Smith, *Italy, A Modern History* (Ann Arbor, 1959), p. 6.

7. John E. Pomfret, with Floyd M. Shumway, *Founding the American Colonies, 1583–1660* (New York, 1970), p. 2.

8. Samuel Eliot Morison, *The Great Explorers: The European Discovery of America* (New York, 1978), p. 74.

9. *Ibid.*, pp. 165, 168.

10. Andrew F. Rolle, *The Immigrant Upraised: Italian Adventurers and Colonists in an Expanding America* (Norman, Okla., 1968), p. 341.

11. Charles Gibson, *Spain in America* (New York, 1966), pp. 199–200.

12. Temple Bodley, *George Rogers Clark: His Life and Public Service* (Boston, 1926), p. 366.

13. James G. Randall, "George Rogers Clark's Service of Supply," *Mississippi Valley Historical Review*, VIII (December 1921), 258.

14. Quoted in John Law, *The Colonial History of Vincennes Under the French, British and American Governments* (Vincennes, 1839), p. 29.

15. *Ibid.*, pp. 21–22.

16. Richard C. Garlick, Jr., "Philip Mazzei," *Italy and the Italians In Washington's Time*, Richard C. Garlick, Jr., et al. (New York, 1933), pp. 6–7.

17. *Virginia Gazette*, 1774–75. Also see *Memoirs of the Life and Peregrinations of the Florentine Philip Mazzei, 1730–1816*, Howard R. Marraro, trans. (New York, 1942), pp. 203–4, for a discussion of the help Jefferson provided in translating Mazzei's writings from Italian into English.

18. Garlick, "Philip Mazzei," p. 18.

19. Margherita Marchione, "Philip Mazzei and the American Revolution," *The United States and Italy: The First Two Hundred Years*, Humbert S. Nelli, ed. (New York, 1977), pp. 10–11.

20. Michael Kraus, *The Atlantic Civilization: Eighteenth-Century Origins* (Ithaca, N.Y., 1949), p. 121.

21. *Memoirs of Mazzei*, p. 413.

22. Howard R. Marraro, "Italo-Americans in Pennsylvania in the Eighteenth Century," *Pennsylvania History*, VII (July 1940), 166.

23. Howard R. Marraro, "Italians in New York During the First Half of the Nineteenth Century," *New York History*, XXVI (July 1945), 282.

24. New York *Herald*, July 25, 1850.

25. Federal Writers' Project of the Works Progress Administration, *The Italians of New York: A Survey* (New York, 1938), p. 12.

Chapter 2: The Land of La Miseria

1. Francesco S. Nitti, *La ricchezza del'Italia* (Naples, 1904), p. 118.

2. Carlo Levi, *Christ Stopped at Eboli* (New York, 1947), pp. 121–22.

3. Quoted in Francis E. Clark, *Our Italian Fellow Citizens in Their Old Homes and Their New* (Boston, 1919), pp. 152–53.

4. Joseph Lopreato, "How Would You Like To Be a Peasant?" *Human Organization*, XXIV (Winter 1965), reprinted in *Peasant*

Society: A Reader, Jack M. Potter et al. (Boston, 1967), p. 425.

5. Quoted in F. G. Friedmann, "The World of 'La Miseria,'" *Partisan Review*, XX (March–April 1953), 220.

6. Joseph Lopreato, *Peasants No More: Social Class and Social Change in an Underdeveloped Society* (San Francisco, 1967), p. 23. This statement was based on the research of Francesco Nitti.

7. Richard Bagot, *Italians of To-Day* 3rd American ed. (Chicago, 1913), p. 33.

8. *Ibid.*, p. 48.

9. "The Spirit of the Mafia," *Fortnightly Review*, 77 (January 1901), 107–8.

10. Denis Mack Smith, *A History of Sicily. Modern Sicily: After 1713* (London, 1968), p. 466. Based on Leonardo Franchetti and Sidney Sonnino, *La Sicilia nel 1876* (2 vol., Florence, 1877).

11. Constance Cronin, *The Sting of Change: Sicilians in Sicily and Australia* (Chicago, 1970), p. 45.

12. Lopreato, "How Would You Like To Be a Peasant?" p. 425.

13. Francis A. J. Ianni, "Familialism in the South of Italy and the United States," *The United States and Italy: The First Two Hundred Years*, Humbert S. Nelli, ed. (New York, 1977), p. 194.

14. Printed in the Louisville *Courier-Journal*, December 14, 1980.

15. Ianni, "Femilialism in the South of Italy and the United States," p. 194.

16. Luigi Bodio, "The Protection of Italian Immigrants in America," *Report of the Commissioner of Education*, II (1894–95), 1789.

17. Robert F. Foerster, *The Italian Emigration of Our Times* (Cambridge, Mass., 1919), pp. 486–87.

18. United States Congress, Senate, *Reports of the Immigration Commission*, IV (Washington, 1911), 153.

19. United States Department of State, *Reports of the Consular Officers of the United States. Emigration and Immigration* (Washington, 1887), p. 253.

20. *Ibid.*, pp. 280 and 290.

21. *Immigration Commission*, pp. 182, 181.

22. *Ibid.*, p. 115.

23. Quoted in Alexander De Conde, *Half Bitter, Half Sweet: An Excursion into Italian-American History* (New York, 1971), p. 72.

24. Broughton Brandenburg, *Imported Americans: The Story of the Experiences of a Disguised American and His Wife Studying the Immigration Question* (New York, 1904), pp. 3, 172.

25. *Ibid*, pp. 175–76.

Chapter 3: The Immigrant Tide

1. Maldwyn Allen Jones, *American Immigration* (Chicago, 1960), p. 93.

2. Robert F. Foerster, "A Statistical Survey of Italian Immigration," *Quarterly Journal of Economics*, XXIII (November 1908), 89.

3. Robert F. Foerster, *The Italian Emigration of Our Times* (Cambridge, Mass., 1919), p. 327.

4. Stefano Miele, "America as a Place To Make Money," *World's Work*, XLI (December 1920), 204.

5. John Foster Carr, "The Coming of the Italian," *Outlook*, LXXXII (February 24, 1906), 422.

6. State of New York, Bureau of Labor Statistics, *Sixteenth Annual Report* (New York and Albany, 1899), p. 1026.

7. Sarah Gertrude Pomeroy, *The Italians* (New York, 1914), p. 41.

8. Francis E. Clark, *Our Italian Fellow Citizens In Their Old Homes and Their New* (Boston, 1919), pp. 191–92.

9. Samuel L. Baily, "The Role of Two Newspapers in the Assimilation of Italians in Buenos Aires and Sao Paulo, 1893–1913," *International Migration Review*, XII (Fall 1978), 324.

10. Cyrus L. Sulzberger, "Immigration," *Proceedings of the National Conference of Charities and Correction, 1912*, p. 245.

11. W. B. Bailey, "The Bird of Passage," *American Journal of Sociology*, XVIII (November 1912), 394.

12. Harry Jerome, *Migration and Business Cycles* (New York, 1926), p. 243.

13. United States Congress, Senate, *Reports of the Industrial Commission* (Washington, 1901), XV, 473.

14. John S. McDonald and Leatrice D. McDonald, "Chain Migration, Ethnic Neighborhood Formation and Social Networks," *Milbank Memorial Fund Quarterly*, 42 (January 1964), p. 88.

15. Richard N. Juliani, "American Voices, Italian Accents: The Perception of Social Conditions and Personal Motives by Immigrants," *Italian Americana*, I (Autumn 1974), 22.

16. Frank P. Sargent, "The Need of Closer Inspection and Greater Restriction of Immigration," *Century Magazine*, LXVII (January 1904), 470.

17. John R. Commons, *Races and Immigrants in America* (New York, 1907), pp. 133, 166.

18. Peter A. Speek, *A Stake in the Land* (New York, 1921), p. 8.

19. *Industrial Commission*, XV, 497.

20. G. E. De Palma Castiglione, "Italian Immigration into the United States, 1901–4," *American Journal of Sociology*, XI (September 1905), p. 204.

21. Giovanni Preziosi, *Gl'italiani negli Stati Uniti del Nord* (Milan, 1909), p. 81.

22. Denis Mack Smith, *A History of Sicily. Modern Sicily: After 1713* (London, 1968), p. 503.

23. Alberto Pecorini, "The Italian as an Agricultural Laborer," *Annals of the American Academy of Political and Social Science*, XXXIII (March 1909), 158.

24. *Industrial Commission*, XIX, 969.

25. Pecorini, "The Italian as an Agricultural Laborer," p. 164.

26. "A Model Italian Colony in Arkansas," *Review of Reviews*, XXXIV (September 1906), 361–62.

27. Anita Moore, "A Safe Way To Get on the Soil," *World's Work*, XXIV (June 1912), 215.

28. John V. Baiamonte, Jr., "Immigrants in Rural America: A Study of the Italians of Tangipahoa Parish, Louisiana," unpublished Ph.D. dissertation, Mississippi State University, 1972, p. 12.

29. George E. Cunningham, "The Italian, A Hindrance to White Solidarity in Louisiana, 1890–1898," *Journal of Negro History*, L (January, 1965), 36.

30. Hans Christian Palmer, "Italian Immigration and the Development of California Agriculture," unpublished Ph.D. dissertation, University of California, Berkeley, 1965, p. 243.

Chapter 4: Italian Immigrants in Urban America

1. John R. Seeley, "The Slum: Its Nature, Use, and Users," *Journal of American Institute of Planners*, XXV (February 1959), 10–12.

2. Antonio Stella, *Some Aspects of Italian Immigration to the United States* (New York, 1924), p. 93.

3. *Real Estate and Builders Guide*, I (June 10, 1893), 905.

4. David Ward, "The Emergence of Central Immigrant Ghettoes in American Cities, 1840–1920," *Annals of the American Association of Geographers*, LVIII (June 1968), 343.

5. New York Association for Improving the Condition of the Poor, *Report for 1857* (New York, 1858).

6. John Palmer Gavit, *Americans by Choice* (New York, 1922), p. 37.

7. John Foster Carr, "The Coming of the Italian," *Outlook*, LXXXII (February 24, 1906), 422.

8. Eliot Lord, John J. D. Trenor, and Samuel J. Barrows, *The Italian in America* (New York, 1905), pp. 77–79.

9. Lillian W. Betts, "The Italian in New York," *University Settlement Studies Quarterly*, I (October 1905), 95.

10. Mary A. Frasca, "Democracy in Immigrant Neighborhood Life," *Proceedings of the National Conference of Social Work, 1920*, pp. 500–501.

11. Thomas Kessner, *The Golden Door: Italian and Jewish Immigrant Mobility in New York City, 1880–1915* (New York, 1977), p. 148.

12. Ralph Foster Weld, *Brooklyn Is America* (New York, 1950), pp. 137–39.

13. Charles W. Churchill, *The Italians of Newark: A Community Study* (New York, 1975), pp. 23–27. This is a reprint of Churchill's Ph.D. dissertation, submitted to New York University in 1942.

14. Raymond Stevenson Dondero, "The Italian Settlement of San Francisco," unpublished M.A. thesis, University of California, Berkeley, 1953, p. 31.

15. Paul Radin, *The Italians of San Francisco: Their Adjustment and Acculturation* (Sacramento, 1935), p. 26.

16. Quoted in Andrew F. Rolle, *The Immigrant Upraised: Italian Adventurers and Colonists in an Expanding America* (Norman, Okla., 1968), p. 255.

17. Deanna Paoli Gumina, *The Italians of San Francisco, 1850–1930* (New York, 1978), p. 19.

18. Jean Ann Scarpaci, "Immigrants in the New South: Italians in Louisiana's Sugar Parishes, 1880–1910," *Studies in Italian American Social History: Essays in Honor of Leonard Covello*, Francesco Covello, ed. (Totowa, N.J., 1975), p. 138.

19. United States Congress, Senate, *Reports of the Industrial Commission* (Washington, 1901), XV, 474.

20. Dondero, "The Italian Settlement of San Francisco," p. 67.

21. Kessner, *The Golden Door*, p. 142.

Chapter 5: The Economic Adjustment

1. Raymond Stevenson Dondero, "The Italian Settlement of San Francisco," unpublished M.A. thesis, University of California, Berkeley, 1953, pp. 76–79.

2. Charles A. Fracchia and George R. Bianchi, "Italian-American Contributions to San Francisco Since 1900," *Italians in California,* Alessandro Buccari, ed. (San Francisco, 1977), p. 56.

3. Frederick H. Wright, *The Italians in America* (New York, 1913), p. 18.

4. Charlotte Adams, "Italian Life in New York," *Harper's Magazine,* LXII (April 1881), 677.

5. Howard R. Marraro, "Italians in New York in the Eighteen Fifties, Part II," *New York History,* XXX (July 1949), 285.

6. *Biographical and Historical Memoirs of Louisiana* (Chicago, 1892), II, 293.

7. Edward Steiner, *On the Trail of the Immigrant* (New York, 1906), p. 262.

8. United States Congress, Senate, *Reports of the Industrial Commission* (Washington, 1901), XV, 432.

9. This and the following paragraph are from Domenick Ciolli, "The Wop in the Track Gang," *The Immigrants in America Review,* II (July 1916), 61–66.

10. United States Congress, Senate, *Reports of the Immigration Commission* (Washington, 1911), II, 392.

11. John Koren, "The Padrone System and Padrone Banks," *United States Department of Labor Bulletin,* IX (March 1897), 115–16.

12. "$10,000,000 Worth of Peanuts," *Fortune* magazine (April 1938), p. 144.

13. From a newspaper ad reproduced in Joseph Giovinco, "Democracy in Banking: The Bank of Italy and California's Italians," *California Historical Society Quarterly,* XLVII (September 1968), 202.

14. S. Merlino, "Italian Immigrants and Their Enslavement," *Forum,* XV (April 1893), 184.

15. Mabel Hurd Willett, *The Employment of Women in the Clothing Trade* (New York, 1902), p. 99.

16. Jacob A. Riis, Robert A. Wood, et al., *The Poor in Great Cities* (New York, 1895), pp. 92–95.

17. Louise C. Odencrantz, *Italian Women in Industry: A Study of Conditions in New York City* (New York, 1919), p. 4.

18. Edwin Fenton, *Immigrants and Unions, A Case Study. Italians and American Labor, 1870–1920* (New York, 1975), p. 214. Originally prepared as a Ph.D. dissertation at Harvard University in 1957.

19. George E. Pozzetta, "The Italians of New York City, 1890–1914," unpublished Ph.D. dissertation, University of North Carolina at Chapel Hill, 1971, p. 359.

20. Edwin Fenton, "Italian Immigrants in the Stoneworkers' Union," *Labor History*, III (Spring 1962), 206–7.

21. Arthur Woods, "The Problem of the Black Hand," *McClure's Magazine*, XXXIII (May 1909), 40.

Chapter 6: Politics and the Ladder of Success

1. William Foote Whyte, *Street Corner Society: The Social Structure of an Italian Slum* (Chicago, 1942), p. 271.

2. *Ibid.*, p. 200.

3. Grace Abbott, *The Immigrant and the Community* (New York, 1917), pp. 256–57.

4. Robert F. Foerster, *The Italian Emigration of Our Times* (Cambridge, Mass., 1919), p. 400.

5. Nick Gentile, *Vita di capomafia* (Rome, 1963), p. 48. Gentile was, himself, an Italian-American criminal leader for more than twenty years.

6. Ralph Foster Weld, *Brooklyn Is America* (New York, 1950), p. 146.

7. John Palmer Gavit, *Americans by Choice* (New York, 1922), p. 364.

8. Federal Writers' Project, Works Progress Administration, *The Italians of New York: A Survey* (New York, 1938), p. 16.

9. George E. Pozzetta, "The Italians of New York City, 1890–1914," unpublished Ph.D. dissertation, University of North Carolina at Chapel Hill, 1971, p. 378.

10. Chicago *L'Italia*, August 24, 1913.

11. *Ibid.*, April 1, 1905.

12. Harold Gosnell, "Non-Naturalization: A Study in Political Assimilation," *American Journal of Sociology*, XXXIII (May 1928), 930–39, and "Characteristics of the Non-Naturalized," *American Journal of Sociology*, XXXIV (March 1929), 847–55; and Charles E. Merriam and Harold F. Gosnell, *Non-Voting: Causes and Methods of Control* (Chicago, 1924), pp. 42–46.

13. John Lombardi, *Labor's Voice in the Cabinet* (New York, 1942), pp. 128–29.

14. William Preston, Jr., *Aliens and Dissenters, Federal Suppression of Radicals, 1903–1933* (Cambridge, Mass., 1963), p. 181.

15. Andrew F. Rolle, *The Immigrant Upraised: Italian Adventurers and Colonists in an Expanding America* (Norman, Okla., 1968), p. 283.

16. Arthur Mann, *La Guardia, A Fighter Against His Times, 1882–1933* (Philadelphia, 1959), p. 21.

17. Howard Zinn, *La Guardia in Congress* (Ithaca, N. Y., 1959), p. 273.

18. Mann, *La Guardia*, p. 62.

19. *Ibid.*, p. 109.

20. Zinn, *La Guardia in Congress*, p. 49.

Chapter 7: The Fabric of Immigrant Life

1. Robert E. Park, "Foreign Language Press and Social Progress," *Proceedings of the National Conference of Social Work, 1920*, p. 494.

2. Constantine M. Panunzio, *The Soul of an Immigrant* (New York, 1922), p. 231.

3. Edith Abbott and Sophonisba P. Breckinridge, *The Delinquent Child and the Home* (New York, 1912), p. 55.

4. Gino C. Speranza, "Many Societies of Italian Colony: Their Uses and Their Abuses Discussed by an Italian Citizen," *New York Times*, March 8, 1903.

5. Edwin Fenton, *Immigrants and Unions, A Case Study: Italians and American Labor, 1870–1920* (New York, 1975), p. 53. Originally prepared as a Ph.D. dissertation, Harvard University, 1957.

6. Luigi Carnovale, *Il Giornalismo degli emigrati italiani nel Nord America* (Chicago, 1908), p. 34.

7. Quoted in Howard R. Marraro, "Italians in New York During the First Half of the Nineteenth Century," *New York History*, XXVI (July 1945), 291.

8. Fenton, *Immigrants and Unions*, p. 49.

9. Caroline F. Ware, *Greenwich Village, 1920–1930: A Comment on American Civilization in the Post-War Years* (New York, 1935), p. 155.

10. Quoted in Commonwealth of Massachusetts, Commission on Immigration, *The Problem of Immigration in Massachusetts* (Boston, 1914), p. 204.

11. "Italian Order Grows," *The Interpreter*, II (February 1923), 13.

12. Ordine Figli d'Italia in America, *Numero Ricordo per la Inaugurazione della Grande Loggia ed Istallazione del Grande Concilio dell'Illinois* (Chicago, 1924), pages unnumbered.

13. Charlotte Kimball, "An Outline of Amusements Among Italians in New York," *Charities*, V (August 18, 1900), 2.

14. Commissariato dell' Emigrazione, *Emigrazione e Colonie, III* (Rome, 1908), 122.

15. A. Richard Sogliuzzo, "Notes for a History of the Italian-American Theatre of New York," *Theatre Survey*, XIV (November 1973), 59.

16. *Ibid.*, pp. 68–69.

17. Deanna Paoli Gumina, *"Connazionali, Stenterello,* and *Farfariello*: Italian Variety Theatre in San Francisco," *California Historical Quarterly*, LIV (Spring 1975), 33.

18. *Ibid.*, p. 27.

19. Elisabeth Irwin, "Where the Players Are Marionettes and the Age of Chivalry Is Born Again in a little Italian Theater in Mulberry Street," *Craftsman*, V (Summer 1907), 667.

20. J. M. Scanland, "An Italian Quarter Mosaic," *Overland Monthly*, XLVII (April 1906), 330.

21. Park, "Foreign Language Press and Social Progress," p. 495.

22. Robert E. Park, *The Immigrant Press and Its Control* (New York, 1922), p. 343.

23. "Among the Foreign-Born," *Bulletin* (subsequently *Interpreter*), I (December 1922), 10.

24. W. H. Agnew, "Pastoral Care of Italian Children in America. Some Plain Facts About the Condition of Our Italian Children," *American Ecclesiastical Review*, XLVIII (March 1913), 258.

25. A. Di Domenica, "The Sons of Italy in America," *Missonary Review of the World, XLI* (March 1918), 193.

Chapter 8: The Family in Italy and America

1. Quoted in William Foote Whyte, "Social Organization in the Slum," *American Sociological Review*, VIII (February 1943), 36.

2. Floyd Mansfield Martinson, *Family in Society* (New York, 1970), p. 88.

3. Luigi Barzini, *The Italians* (New York, 1964), p. 198.

4. Quoted in William C. McCready, "The Persistence of Ethnic Variation in American Families," *Ethnicity in the United States: A Preliminary Reconnaissance*, Andrew M. Greeley (New York, 1974), p. 160.

5. Leonard Covello, *The Social Background of the Italo-American School Child: A Study of the Southern Italian Family Mores and Their Effect on the School Situation in Italy and America* (Leiden, Netherlands, 1967), p. 154.

6. Quoted in Charlotte G. Chapman, *Milocca: A Sicilian Village* (Cambridge, Mass., 1971), p. 124.

7. Covello, *The Social Background of the Italo-American School Child*, pp. 213–14.

8. Quoted in Robert E. Park and Herbert A. Miller, *Old World Traits Transplanted* (New York, 1921), p. 11.

9. Covello, *The Social Background of the Italo-American School Child*, p. 196.

10. *Ibid.*, pp. 175–76.

11. Francis A. J. Ianni, "Familialism in the South of Italy and in the United States," *The United States and Italy: The First Two Hundred Years*, Humbert S. Nelli, ed. (New York, 1977), p. 194.

12. Paul Campisi, "Ethnic Family Patterns: The Italian Family in the United States," *American Journal of Sociology*, LIII (May 1948), 448.

13. Francis A. J. Ianni, "The Italo-American Teen-Ager," *The Annals of the American Academy of Political and Social Science*, 338 (November 1961), p. 74.

14. Elizabeth H. Pleck, "A Mother's Wages: Income Earning Among Married Italian and Black Women, 1896–1911," *The American Family in Social-Historical Perspective*, Michael Gordon, ed., 2nd ed. (New York, 1978), p. 492.

15. Caroline F. Ware, *Greenwich Village, 1920–1930: A Comment on American Civilization in the Post-War Years* (New York, 1935), p. 182.

16. Ida L. Hull, "Special Problems in Italian Families," *Proceedings of the National Conference of Social Work, 1924*, p. 291.

17. Philip M. Rose, *The Italians in America* (New York, 1922), p. 77 and *Immigration Journal*, September 1916, pp. 88–93.

18. Ware, *Greenwich Village*, p. 181.

19. Michael Lalli, "The Italian-American Family: Assimilation and Change, 1900–1965," *The Family Coordinator*, XVIII (January 1969), 46.

20. Nathan Glazer and Daniel Patrick Moynihan, *Beyond the Melting Pot: The Negroes, Puerto Ricans, Jews, Italians, and Irish in New York City* 2nd ed. (Cambridge, Mass., 1970), p. 199.

21. Robert E. Park, "Immigrant Heritages," *Proceedings of the National Conference of Social Work, 1921*, p. 496.

22. Campisi, "Ethnic Family Patterns: The Italian in the United States," p. 447.

23. *Ibid.*

24. Bartolomeo J. Palisi, "Ethnic Generation and Family Structure," *Journal of Marriage and the Family*, XXVIII (February 1966), 50.

25. Campisi, "Ethnic Family Patterns: The Italian in the United States," p. 449.

Chapter 9: The Interwar Years

1. William E. Leuchtenburg, *The Perils of Prosperity, 1914–32* (Chicago, 1958), p. 208.

2. Quoted in Herbert B. Ehrmann, *The Case That Will Not Die: Commonwealth vs. Sacco and Vanzetti* (Boston, 1969), p. 472.

3. Felix Frankfurter, *The Case of Sacco and Vanzetti: A Critical Analysis for Lawyers and Laymen* (Boston, 1927), p. 8.

4. G. Louis Joughin and Edmund M. Morgan, *The Legacy of Sacco and Vanzetti* (New York, 1948), p. 94.

5. Lawrence Frank Pisani, *The Italian in America. A Social Study and History* (New York, 1957), p. 196.

6. Quoted in Gaetano Salvemini and George La Piana, *What To Do with Italy* (New York, 1943), pp. 63, 64, 74.

7. Laura Fermi, *Illustrious Immigrants: The Intellectual Migration From Europe, 1930–41*, 2nd ed. (Chicago, 1971), p. 388.

8. Deanna Paoli Gumina, *The Italians of San Francisco, 1850–1930* (New York, 1978), p. 189.

9. Federal Writers' Project of the Works Progress Administration, *The Italians of New York: A Survey* (New York, 1938), p. 171.

10. Larry Fox, *Illustrated History of Basketball* (New York, 1974), p. 67.

11. Neil Isaacs, *All the Moves: A History of College Basketball* (Philadelphia, 1975), p. 113.

12. New York *Times*, September 21, 1947.

13. Melvin G. Holli and Peter D'A. Jones, *American Mayors*, in press.

14. V. O. Key, Jr., *Southern Politics in State and Nation* (New York, 1950), p. 163.

15. Edward F. Haas, "New Orleans on the Half-Shell: The Maestri Era, 1936–1946," *Louisiana History*, XIII (Summer 1972), 289.

16. Samuel Lubell, *The Future of American Politics*, 3rd ed. rev. (New York, 1965), p. 54.

17. Warren Moscow, *What Have You Done for Me Lately? The Ins and Outs of New York City Politics* (Englewood Cliffs, N. J., 1967), p. 169.

Notes

207

Chapter 10: The Emergence of the Ethnic Italian

1. Arthur Link, *American Epoch: A History of the United States since the 1890's*, 3rd ed. (New York, 1967), p. 669.

2. Quoted in Barbara Mikulski, "The Ethnic Neighborhood: Leave Room for a Boccie Ball," *Pieces of a Dream: the Ethnic Worker's Crisis with America*, Michael Wenk, S. M. Tomasi, and Geno Baroni, eds. (New York, 1972), p. 56.

3. Quoted in Edward C. Banfield, *The Unheavenly City Revisited: A Revision of the Unheavenly City* (Boston, 1973), p. 15.

4. *Fra Noi* (Chicago), November 1971.

5. Ken Auletta, *The Streets Were Paved With Gold* (New York, 1980), p. 226.

6. John Fante, "The Odyssey of a Wop," quoted in Richard Krickus, *Pursuing the American Dream: White Ethnics and the New Populism* (Garden City, N. Y., 1976), p. 93.

7. Spencer Di Scala, "The Boston Italian-American Community," *The United States and Italy: The First Two Hundred Years*, Humbert S. Nelli, ed. (New York, 1977), p. 229.

8. *Ibid.*

9. Chicago *Tribune*, August 22, 1976.

10. Nathan Glazer and Daniel Patrick Moynihan, *Beyond the Melting Pot: The Negroes, Puerto Ricans, Jews, Italians, and Irish of New York City*, 2nd ed. (Cambridge, Mass., 1970), pp. 204–5.

11. Francis A. J. Ianni, "The Italian-American Teen-Ager," *Annals of the American Academy of Political and Social Science*, 338 (November 1961), p. 77.

12. Joseph Lopreato, *Italian Americans* (New York, 1970), pp. 85–86.

13. *Fra Noi* (Chicago), September, 1981.

14. Mario Puzo, "The Italians, American Style," *The New York Times Magazine*, August 6, 1967, pp. 28–29.

15. Nicholas Acocella, "Politics: Who Are We Now?" *Attenzione*, I (July 1979), 22.

16. Edward J. Miranda, "The Italian-Americans: Who, What, Where, When, Why," *Identity*, I (July 1977), 15.

17. Fred Barbaro, "Ethnic Affirmation, Affirmative Action, and the Italian-American," *Italian Americana*, I (Autumn 1974), 46.

18. Andrew M. Greeley, *Ethnicity in the United States: A Preliminary Reconnaissance* (New York, 1974), p. 51.

19. Glazer and Moynihan, *Beyond the Melting Pot*, p. 206.

20. John Mariani, "The Four Horsemen and the Apocalypse," *Attenzione*, I (July 1979), 44.

21. New York *Times*, June 4, 1978.

22. Peter Marris, "A Report on Urban Renewal in the United States," *The Urban Condition: People and Policy in the Metropolis*, Leonard J. Duhl, ed. (New York, 1963), p. 126.

23. Earl Wilson, *Sinatra: An Unauthorized Biography* (New York, 1977), p. 37.

24. Chicago *Sun-Times*, August 22, 1981.

25. *Kirkus Review*, XLIX (April 1, 1976), 458.

26. Wilson, *Sinatra*, p. 71.

27. Ralph Salerno and John S. Tompkins, *The Crime Confederation: Cosa Nostra and Allied Operations in Organized Crime* (Garden City, N. Y., 1969), p. 207.

28. Warren Moscow, *What Have You Done for Me Lately? The Ins and Outs of New York City Politics* (Englewood Cliffs, N. J., 1967), p. 176.

29. Gay Talese, "The Ethnics of Frank Costello," *Esquire* (September 1961), p. 143.

30. Moscow, *What Have You Done for Me Lately?*, pp. 176, 179.

31. Samuel Lubell, "Rhode Island's Little Firecracker," *Saturday Evening Post*, CCXXII (November 12, 1949), 178.

32. Andrew M. Greeley, *Why Can't They Be Like Us? America's White Ethnic Groups* (New York, 1975), p. 15.

33. Washington *Post*, October 11, 1976.

Bibliographical Note

The literature on Italian immigration is vast but uneven in quality and value to the student of the Italian-American experience. Therefore only the more significant or useful books, articles, and published reports printed in English are given here. Although many of the studies listed below cover more than one topic they are mentioned only once in order to keep the bibliography within manageable limits.

The Italian background and factors influencing emigration are examined in Jeremy Boissevan, "Poverty and Politics in a Sicilian Agro-Town," *International Archives of Ethnography*, V 50, Pt. 2 (1966), pp. 198–236; Joseph Lopreato, *Peasants No More: Social Class and Social Change in an Underdeveloped Society* (San Francisco, 1967) and "Social Stratification and Mobility in a South Italian Town," *American Sociological Review*, XXVI (August 1961), 585–96; Bolton King and Thomas Okey, *Italy To-Day*, New and Enlarged ed. (London, 1909); Denis Mack Smith, *A History of Sicily. Modern Sicily: After 1713* (London, 1968); F. G. Friedman, "The World of 'La Miseria,'" *Partisan Review*, XX (March–April 1953), 218–31; Edward C. Banfield, *The Moral Basis of a Backward Society* (Glencoe, Ill., 1958); Henner Hess, *Mafia and Mafiosi: The Structure of Power* (Lexington, Mass., 1973); Anton Blok, *The Mafia of a Sicilian Village, 1860–1960: A Study of Violent Peasant Entrepreneurs* (Oxford, 1974); J. S. McDonald, "Italy's Rural Social Structure and Emigration," *Occidente*, XII (September–October 1956), 437–56; Grazia Dore, "Some Social and Historical Aspects of Italian Emigration to America," *Journal of Social History*, II (Winter 1968), 95–122. Phyllis H. Williams, *South Italian Folkways in Europe and America* (New Haven, 1938); Leonard Covello, "The Social Background of the Italo-American School Child, A Study of the Southern Italian Family Mores and Their Effect on the School Situation in Italy and America," unpublished Ph.D. dissertation, New York University, 1944, revised by the author and published in Leiden in 1967.

Robert F. Foerster's classic study, *The Italian Emigration of Our Times* (Cambridge, Mass., 1919) devotes five chapters (of a total of twenty-four) to the Italian background and four specifically to immigration to the United States. Unfortunately, it is out-of-date both in source materials and conceptual framework. Foerster made no use of a variety of primary works which immigration scholars and urban specialists have found to be valuable, such as foreign-language newspapers, fraternal organization and Catholic parish records, precinct voting records, manuscript census materials, and city directories. Although the rural experience of Italians in America was of minor importance compared with the urban, Foerster devoted an entire chapter to the former which treating the latter only incidentally in other chapters. The emphasis throughout is on economic factors, while political, social, and cultural influences are either ignored or unrecognized.

Among the numerous general studies of Italian immigration are Eliot Lord, John J. D. Trenor, and Samuel J. Barrows, *The Italian in America* (New York, 1905); Philip M. Rose, *The Italian in America* (New York, 1922); Francis E. Clark, *Our Italian Fellow Citizens in Their Old Homes and Their New* (Boston, 1919); Antonio Stella, *Some Aspects of Italian Immigration to the United States* (New York, 1924); Lawrence F. Pisani, *The Italian in America* (New York, 1957). Joseph Lopreato, *Italian Americans* (New York, 1970), is a sociological study; Luciano J. Iorizzo and Salvatore Mondello, *The Italian-Americans* (New York, 1971), emphasizes the experience in small eastern cities; Andrew Rolle, *The Italian Americans: Troubled Roots* (New York, 1980) is an effort "to fuse psychoanalysis with history;" Alexander De Conde, *Half Bitter, Half Sweet: An Excursion into Italian-American History* (New York, 1971), by a leading American diplomatic historian, emphasizes relations between the United States and Italy. One of the many strengths of the book is an extensive bibliographic essay on Italian immigration. Francesco Cordasco and Eugene Bucchioni, eds., *The Italians: Social Backgrounds of an American Group* (Clifton, N. J., 1974), is a selection of articles that focus on the era of large-scale immigration.

Municipal, state, and federal government units and agencies in the United States devoted a great deal of attention to conditions in Italian immigrant colonies. Among the more useful reports are Frank O. Beck, "The Italian in Chicago," *Bulletin of the Department of Public Welfare of Chicago*, II (February 1919), 2–12; Commonwealth of Massachusetts, Commission on Immigration, *The Problem of Immigration in Massachusetts* (Boston, 1914); State of New York; *Report of the*

Commission on Immigration (Albany, 1909); U.S. Commissioner of
Labor, *Seventh Special Report. The Slums of Baltimore, Chicago, New
York and Philadelphia* (1894) and *Ninth Special Report. The Italian
in Chicago, A Social and Economic Study* (1897); U.S. Congress, *Re-
port on Importation of Contract Labor*, 2 Vols. (1889) and *Reports of
the Industrial Commission*, XV (1901), 473–92; U.S. Senate, *Reports
of the Immigration Commission*, 41 Vols. (1911), especially XXVI and
XXVII, "Immigrants in Cities." In the years since its publication, the
Immigration (or Dillingham) Commission *Reports* have received much
criticism, most notably from Isaac A. Hourwich, *Immigration and
Labor: The Economic Aspects of European Immigration to the United
States* (New York, 1912), and Oscar Handlin, *Race and Nationality
in American Life* (Boston, 1957), chap. V, "Old Immigrants and New."
Criticism has centered on the restrictionist bias of the commission and
its interpretation of data. Used with care, however, materials presented
in the *Reports* can be of value.
  The role of Italians in the United States prior to the large-scale
immigration has largely been ignored by scholars. A major exception
was Columbia University Professor Howard R. Marraro who publica-
tions include "Italo-Americans in Pennsylvania in the Eighteenth Cen-
tury," *Pennsylvania History*, VII (July 1940), 159–66; "Italians in New
York During the First Half of the Nineteenth Century," *New York
History*, XXVI (July 1945), 278–305; "Italo-Americans in Eighteenth
Century New York," *New York History*, XVI (July 1940), 316–23;
"Italians in New York in the Eighteen Fifties," reprinted from *New
York History*, April, July, 1949. Material on the early New York
Italian colony is also presented in Charles Loring Brace, *The Danger-
ous Classes of New York and Twenty Years' Work Among Them* (New
York, 1872); Robert Ernst, *Immigrant Life in New York, 1825–1863*
(New York, 1948); Francesco Moncada, "New York's 'Little Italy,' "
Atlanica (April 1937), pp. 14–15, 24. Andrew Rolle has written about
Italian explorers and travelers as well as more permanent settlers in
*The Immigrant Upraised: Italian Adventurers and Colonists in an Ex-
panding America* (Norman, Okla., 1968) and "The Italian Moves
Westward," *Montana: The Magazine of Western History*, XVI (Winter
1966), 13–24. For discussions of the experience of the limited number
of Italians in America during the colonial period see Richard C. Garlick, Jr., *Philip Mazzei, Friend of Jefferson: His Life and Letters* (Baltimore, 1933); *Memoirs of the Life and Peregrinations of the Florentine Philip Mazzei, 1730–1816*, Howard R. Marraro, trans. (New
York, 1942); Margherita Marchione, "Philip Mazzei and the American

Revolution," *The United States and Italy: The First Two Hundred Years*, Humbert S. Nelli, ed. (New York, 1977), pp. 3–12; Richard C. Garlick, et al., *Italy and Italians in Washington's Time* (New York, 1933); Bruno Roselli; *Vigo, A Forgotton Builder of the American Republic* (Boston, 1933); Giovanni E. Schiavo, *The Italians in America Before the Civil War* (New York, 1934).

The process of immigration to the United States in the decades after 1880 is discussed in G. E. Di Palma Castiglione, "Italian Immigration Into the United States, 1901–4," *American Journal of Sociology*, XI (September 1905), 183–206; John S. McDonald and Leatrice D. Mcdonald, "Chain Migration, Ethnic Neighborhood Formation and Social Networks," *Millbank Memorial Fund Quarterly*, XLII (January 1964), 82–97; Robert F. Foerster, "A Statistical Survey of Italian Immigration," *Quarterly Journal of Economics*, XXIII (November 1908), 66–103; Joseph H. Senner, "Immigration from Italy," *North American Review*, CLXII (June 1896), 649–57; W. B. Bailey, "The Bird of Passage," *American Journal of Sociology*, XVIII (November 1912), 391–97; Harry Jerome, *Migration and Business Cycles* (New York, 1926).

Numerous books and articles have been written about the Italian immigrants in New York and Chicago but the experience in New Orleans and San Francisco has largely been ignored. Among the more useful studies are: Federal Writers' Project, Works Progress Administration, *The Italians of New York: A Survey* (New York, 1938); Caroline F. Ware, *Greenwich Village, 1920–1930: A Comment on American Civilization in the Post-War Years* (Boston, 1935); Thomas Kessner, *The Golden Door: Italian and Jewish Immigrant Mobility in New York City, 1880–1915* (New York, 1977); Lillian W. Betts, "The Italian in New York," *University Settlement Studies Quarterly*, I (October 1905), 90–105; Charlotte Adams, "Italian Life in New York," *Harper's Magazine*, LXII (April 1881); John Foster Carr, "The Coming of the Italian," *Outlook*, LXXXII (February 24, 1906), 419–31; William B. Shedd, "The Italian Population in New York City, *Casa Italiana Educational Bulletin*, No. 7 (New York, 1936); Thomas J. Jones, *Sociology of a New York City Block* (New York, 1908); Humbert S. Nelli, *Italians in Chicago, 1880–1930: A Study in Ethnic Mobility* (New York, 1970); Harvey W. Zorbaugh, *The Gold Coast and the Slum* (Chicago, 1929); Alessandro Mastro-Valerio, "Remarks Upon the Italian Colony in Chicago," *Hull House Maps and Papers* (New York, 1895), pp. 131–39; Grace P. Norton, "Chicago Housing Conditions, VII: Two Italian Districts," *American Journal of Sociology*, XVIII (January 1913), 509–42; Natalie Walker, "Chicago Housing Condition, X.

Greeks and Italians in the Neighborhood of Hull House," *American Journal of Sociology*, XXI (November 1915), 285–316; Giovanni E. Schiavo, *The Italians in Chicago: A Study in Americanization* (Chicago, 1928); Paul Radin, *The Italians of San Francisco: Their Adjustment and Acculturation* (Sacramento, 1935); Deanna Paoli Gumina, *The Italians of San Francisco, 1850–1930* (New York, 1978); Humbert S. Nelli, "The Hennessy Murder and the Mafia in New Orleans," *Italian Quarterly*, XIX (Winter–Spring 1976), 77–95; Eleanor Mc-Main, "Behind the Yellow Fever in Little Palermo," *Charities and the Commons*, XV (November 4, 1905), 152–59, on the Italian colony of New Orleans. Studies of Italians in other cities include Blake Mc-Kelvey, "The Italians of Rochester, An Historical Review," *Rochester History*, XXII (October 1960), 1–24; Frederick A. Bushee, "Italian Immigrants in Boston," *Arena*, XVII (April 1897), 722–34; Walter I. Firey, *Land Use in Central Boston* (Cambridge, Mass., 1947), chap. V; Charles W. Churchill, *The Italians of Newark* (New York, 1946); Joan Younger Dickinson, "Aspects of Italian Immigration to Philadelphia," *Pennsylvania Magazine of History and Biography*, XC (October 1966), 445–65; Charles W. Coulter, *The Italians of Cleveland* (Cleveland, 1919); George La Piana, *The Italians in Milwaukee, Wisconsin* (Milwaukee, 1915).

The following paragraphs provide a sampling of the extensive available literature dealing with the padrone system, organized labor, syndicate crime, politics, education, the family, fraternal societies, the press, and religion.

On the padrone system: John Koren, "The Padrone System and Padrone Banks," *U.S. Bureau of Labor Bulletin*, No. 9 (March 1897), pp. 113–29; Frank J. Sheridan, "Italian, Slavic and Hungarian Unskilled Immigrant Laborers in the United States," *U.S. Bureau of Labor Bulletin*, No. 72 (September 1907), pp. 403–86; Dominick Ciolli, "The Wop in the Track Gang," *Immigrants in America Review*, II (July 1916), 61–64. The foregoing are contemporary accounts of the padrone labor system. A more recent effort to evaluate the contributions of the labor agent to American business as well as to immigrant workers is Humbert S. Nelli, "The Italian Padrone System in the United States," *Labor History*, V (Spring 1964), 153–67. Italians and labor have been examined in two excellent articles written by Edwin Fenton, "Italians in the Labor Movement," *Pennsylvania History* XXVI (April 1959), 113–48 and "Italian Workers in the Stonecutters Union," *Labor History*, III (Spring 1962), 188–207 as well as in Fenton's reprinted Ph.D. dissertation, *Immigrants and Unions, A Case*

Study. Italians and American Labor, 1870–1920 (New York, 1975).
Other useful studies are Charles B. Barnes, *The Longshoremen* (New
York, 1915); Ann Withington, "The Lawrence Strike," *Life and Labor*,
II (March 1912), 73–77; Peter Roberts, *The New Immigration* (New
York, 1911); John J. D'Alessandre, "Occupational Trends of Italians
in New York City," *Casa Italiana Educational Bulletin*, No. 8 (New
York, 1935); Alice Henry, *The Trade Union Woman* (New York,
1917); Louise C. Odencrantz, *Italian Women in Industry* (New York,
1919).

Among the many works concerning syndicate crime are Humbert S.
Nelli, *The Business of Crime: Italians and Syndicate Crime in the
United States* (New York, 1976) and "Italians and Crime in Chicago:
The Formative Years, 1890–1920," *American Journal of Sociology*,
LXXIV (January 1969), 373–91; Peter Maas, *The Valachi Papers*
(New York, 1969); Joseph L. Albini, *The American Mafia: Genesis of
a Legend* (New York, 1971); Fred D. Pasley, *Al Capone: The Bi-
ography of a Self-Made Man* (New York, 1930); John Kobler, *Ca-
pone: The Life and World of Al Capone* (New York, 1971); John
Landesco, *Organized Crime in Chicago: Part III of the Illinois Crime
Survey, 1929* (Chicago, 1929; reissued 1968); Craig Thompson and
Allen Raymond, *Gang Rule in New York: The Story of a Lawless Era*
(New York, 1940); Gay Talese, *Honor Thy Father* (New York, 1971);
Vincent Teresa, *My Life in the Mafia* (Garden City, N. Y., 1973);
Raymond Martin, *Revolt in the Mafia* (New York, 1964); Hank Mes-
sick, *The Silent Syndicate* (New York, 1967); Staff and Editors of
Newsday, The Heroin Trail (New York, 1974); and the excellent study
by Francis A. J. Ianni with Elizabeth Reuss-Ianni, *A Family Business:
Kinship and Social Control in Organized Crime* (New York, 1972).

Political activities of immigrants and their children are described in
the following: Humbert S. Nelli, "John Powers and the Italians: Poli-
tics in a Chicago Ward, 1896–1921," *Journal of American History*,
LVII (June 1970), 67–84; Fiorello H. La Guardia, *The Making of an
Insurgent: An Autobiography* (Philadelphia, 1948); Arthur Mann, *La
Guardia: A Fighter Against His Times, 1882–1933* (Philadephia,
1959); and *La Guardia Comes to Power: 1933* (Philadelphia, 1965);
John Palmer Gavit, *Americans by Choice* (New York, 1922); Samuel
Lubell, *The Future of American Politics*, 3rd ed. rev. (New York,
1965), chap. iv and "Rhode Island's Little Firecracker," *Saturday
Evening Post*, CCXXII (November 12, 1949), 31, 174–78 for a sketch
of John D. Pastore; Michael J. Parenti, "Ethnic Politics and the Persistence of Ethnic Identification," *American Political Science Review*,

LXI (September 1967), 717–26; Salvatore J. La Gumina, "Ethnicity in American Political Life: The Italian-American Experience," *International Migration Review*, III (Spring 1969), 78–81; *I Vote My Conscience: Debates, Speeches and Writings of Vito Marcantonio, 1935–1950*, Annette T. Rubinstein, ed. (New York, 1956).

Education among Italian Americans is examined by Jane Addams, "Foreign-born Children in the Primary Grades: Italian Families in Chicago," *National Education Association. Journal of Proceedings and Addresses*, XXXVI (1897), 104–12; Ellen May, "Italian Education and Immigration," *Education*, No. 28 (March 1908), pp. 450–53; Angelo Patri, *A School Master in the Great City* (New York, 1917); Leonard P. Ayres, *Laggards in Our Schools* (New York, 1909); Leonard Covello, "A High School in Its Immigrant Community," *Journal of Educational Sociology*, IX (February 1936), 333–46; Leonard Covello and Guido D'Agostino, *The Heart Is the Teacher* (New York, 1958); Joseph W. Tait, *Some Aspects of the Effect of the Dominant American Culture Upon Children of Italian-Born Parents* (New York, 1942).

For the Italian-American Family: Paul J. Campisi, "Ethnic Family Patterns: The Italian Family in the United States," *American Journal of Sociology*, LIII (May 1948), 443–49; Francis A. J. Ianni, "The Italo-American Teen-Ager," *Annals of the American Academy of Political and Social Science*, V. 338 (November 1961), pp. 70–78; Bartolomeo J. Palisi, "Ethnic Generation and Family Structure," *Journal of Marriage and the Family*, XXVIII (February 1966), 49–50 and "Patterns of Social Participation in a Two-Generation Sample of Italian-Americans," *Sociological Quarterly*, VII (Spring 1966), 163–78; Michael Lalli "The Italian-American Family: Assimilation and Change, 1900–1965," *The Family Coordinator*, XVIII (January 1969), 44–48; Lydio F. Tomasi, *The Italian American Family* (Staten Island, N. Y., N.D.); Elizabeth H. Pleck, "A Mother's Wages: Income Earning Among Married Italian and Black Women, 1896–1911," *The American Family in Social-Historical Perspective*, Michael Gorden, ed., 2nd ed. (New York, 1978), pp. 490–510; William Foote Whyte, *Street Corner Society* (Chicago, 1943); Herbert J. Gans, *The Urban Villagers: Group and Class in the Life of Italian Americans* (New York, 1962).

Studies dealing with immigrant community institutions include Robert E. Park, *The Immigrant Press and Its Control* (New York, 1922); George E. Pozzetta, "The Italian Immigrant Press of New York City: The Early Years, 1880–1915," *Journal of Ethnic Studies*, I (Fall 1973), 32–46; Humbert S. Nelli, "Chicago's Italian-Language Press and World War I," *Studies in Italian American Social History: Essays in Honor of Leonard Covello*, Francesco Cordasco, ed. (Totowa, N. J., 1975), pp. 66–80; A. Richard Sogliuzzo, "Notes For a History of the Italian-American Theatre of New York," *Theatre Survey*, XIV (November 1973), 59–75; Charlotte Kimball, "An Outline of Amusements Among Italians in New York City," *Charities*, V (August 18, 1900), 1–8; Deanna Paoli Gumina, "*Connazionali, Stenterello*, and *Farfariello*: Italian Variety Theater in San Francisco," *California Historical Quarterly*, LIV (Spring 1975), 27–36; Jeanette Sayre Smith, "Broadcasting for Marginal Americans," *Public Opinion Quarterly*, VI (Winter 1942), 588–603; Antonio Mangano, "The Associated Life of the Italians in New York City," *Charities*, XII (May 7, 1904), 476–82; Henry J. Browne, "The 'Italian Problem' in the United States, 1880–1900," *U.S. Catholic Historical Society, Historical Records and Studies*, XXXV (1946), 46–72; Francis X. Femminella, "The Impact of Italian Migration and American Catholicism," *American Catholic Sociological Review*, XXII (Fall 1961), 233–41; Silvano M. Tomasi, *Piety and Power: The Role of the Italian Parishes in the New York Metropolitan Area, 1880–1930* (New York, 1975).

On the rise of "the new ethnicity" in the period since the mid-1960s see: Nathan Glazer and Daniel P. Moynihan, *Beyond the Melting Pot: The Negroes, Puerto Ricans, Jews, Italians, and Irish of New York City*, 2nd ed., (Cambridge, Mass., 1970); Patrick J. Gallo, *Ethnic Alienation: The Italian-Americans* (Rutherford, N. J., 1974); Richard Gambino, *Blood of My Blood: The Dilemma of the Italian-Americans* (Garden City, N. Y., 1974); Alfred Aversa, Jr., "Italian Neo-Ethnicity: The Search for Self-Identity," *Journal of Ethnic Studies*, VI (Summer 1978), 49–56; Fred Barbaro, "Ethnic Affirmation, Affirmative Action, and the Italian-American," *Italian Americana*, I (Autumn 1974), 41–58. More general studies on the white ethnic movement include Andrew M. Greeley, *Ethnicity in the United States: A Preliminary Reconnaissance* (New York, 1974), and *Why Can't They Be Like Us? America's White Ethnic Groups* (New York, 1975); Stanley Feldstein and Lawrence Costello, eds., *The Ordeal of Assimilation: A Documentary History of the White Working Class, 1830's to the 1970's* (Garden City, N. Y., 1974); Richard Krickus, *Pursuing the American Dream: White Ethnics and the New Populism* (Garden City, N. Y., 1976); Michael Novak, *The Rise of the Unmeltable Ethnics: The New Political Force of the Seventies* (New York, 1971).

Index

(Prepared by Virginia Althoff)

Borsieri, Pietro, 17
Bossism, *see* Padrone system
Boston, 62, 64, 116, 175–78, 188
Bottari, Vic, 164
Brandenburg, Broughton, 34–35
Brazil, 31–32, 43, 161
Breckenridge, Sophonisba P., 115
Brisson, Freddie, 189
Brovelli, Angel, 164
Buenos Aires, 43–44
Buffalo, New York, 178, 180
Butler, Nicholas Murray, 156

Cabot, John, 5
Calabria, 21, 27, 65
California: agriculture in, 54; immigration to, 31, 47, 67; Italian-Americans in, 40, 54, 73–74, 160
Caminetti, Anthony, 108–9
Campania, 24, 65
Campanini, Cleofante, 122
Camphausen, Edward, 32
Campisi, Paul, 136, 143, 149–50
Canada, 22, 79
Capelli, Louis W., 192
Capone, Al, 103, 106, 160, 163, 191
Capra, Frank, 187–88
Carideo, Frank, 164
Carnovale, Luigi, 116
Carr, John Foster, 63
Carroll, Philip, 32
Caruso, Enrico, 122
Casali, G. F. Secchi de, 123
Castiglia, Francesco, *see* Costello, Frank
Castiglioni, Count Luigi, 18
Catholic Church, 6, 116, 144; Irish domination of, in United States, 119, 127–28, 179–80; in Italy, 8, 20, 26, 256
Ceppi, Charles, 164
Chaplin, Charlie, 121
Charities, 118
Chicago, 58, 64, 96, 182; Italian-American community in, 41, 59,

61–62, 75–76, 175–78; Italian-American press, 116, 123–25; job availability in, 47, 87, 91; padrones in, 78–79; political machine in, 86, 94, 98, 101, 103, 107; suburbs of, 70, 159
Chicago Commons Settlement House, 59
Chicago *Tribune*, 176, 187
Children's Aid Society, 75
Chinese Exclusion Bill, 109
Chino, Father Eusebio, 6
Chitti, Luigi, 17
Churchill, Charles, 65
Churchill, Winston, 157
Cimino, Michael, 186
Ciolli, Dominick, 80
Circolo filodrammatico Italo-Americano, 120
City University of New York, 184, 186
Ciuci, Henry, 164
Clark, George Rogers, 9–10
Clark, Rev. N. Walling, 32–33
Cleveland, 47, 62, 178
Colle, Virginia, 12–13
Colombo, Joe, 190
Colombo, Russ, 163
Colosimo, Jim, 95, 103
Columbia University, 17, 83
Columbus, Christopher, 3–5
Commissariato Generale della Emigrazione (Bureau of Emigration), 30
Commons, John R., 47
Compagnia filodrammatica napoletana, 120
Compagnia Galileo Galilei, 120
Connecticut, 7, 51
Conte, Richard, 188
Coppola, Francis Ford, 186
Corbin, Austin, 52
Costello, Frank, 163, 190–91
Coughlin, "Bathhouse John," 95, 103
Covello, Leonard, 24–25, 132, 135

Index